2ND EDITION

The Mass
of the
Early Christians

2ND EDITION

The Mass of the Early Christians

Mike Aquilina

Our Sunday Visitor Publishing Division
Our Sunday Visitor, Inc.
Huntington, Indiana 46750

Copyright © 2001, 2007 by
Our Sunday Visitor Publishing Division

26 25 24 23 22   8 9 10 11 12

Our Sunday Visitor Publishing Division
Our Sunday Visitor, Inc.
200 Noll Plaza
Huntington, IN 46750

ISBN: 978-1-59276-320-7 (Inventory No. T419)
RELIGION/Christianity/Theology/History; RELIGION/
Christianity/Rituals & Practice; RELIGION/Christianity/
Catholicism
LCCN: 2007926197

Cover art: A fifth-century mosaic of loaves and fishes, found in the remains of a Byzantine church in Tabgha, Israel, the traditional site of Jesus' feeding of the 5,000 (Mk 6:41)

Cover design by Rebecca J. Heaston
Interior design by Sherri L. Hoffman

For Witt Yeagley and David Scott,
my editors first and foremost.

Table of Contents

Foreword

A sked to name a concept that defines the work of the Second Vatican Council, most people would likely mention *aggiornamento*, a word commonly translated as "bringing up to date." This is often considered to have been the sole task of the council, and perhaps nowhere was that project of updating more clearly seen than in the revisions of the liturgical life of the Church, specifically the introduction of the *novus ordo*, or Missal of Pope Paul VI.

And yet, if *aggiornamento* was a fundamental task of the council that met in Rome (1962-1965), then just as important in the mind of the council fathers was *ressourcement*, a word that can be rendered as "recovery of the sources." For if the life and teaching of the Church were to be brought more fully into dialogue with the modern age, then, it was thought, one of the best ways to do that was by reacquainting the Church universal with the roots and foundations of her theology, and the way that belief had been lived and prayed. Indeed, the Liturgical Movement — which had been active in the Church for much of the twentieth century and had prepared the way for the conciliar reflections on the liturgy — championed a retrieval of the liturgical witness of the Church's earliest centuries.

What you hold in your hands is an excellent compendium of documents testifying to that earliest belief and practice. By reading these well-chosen excerpts from the Church Fathers (and even from heretics and enemies of the Church!), you will gain a renewed appreciation for the Mass, which the council sought to renew and make accessible to the faithful in our present age. These texts are a call to the children of the Church, at this dawn of a new millennium, to reverence the awesome gift of the Body and Blood of the Lord and celebrate the Eucharist as the source of our unity as his people. Such an undertaking is all the more necessary at a time when it is widely reported that many Catholics have lost an appreciation for the sacredness of the liturgy and have become confused over the Real Presence of Christ in the Eucharist.

In reading and meditating on these texts, however, we must be careful to avoid a kind of romanticism that would see them merely as a "blueprint" for the liturgy in our own day and age. As Pope Pius XII wisely instructed in his encyclical *Mediator Dei*: "Ancient usage must not be esteemed more suitable and proper . . . on the simple ground that it carries the savor and aroma of antiquity." To attempt a "restoration" of the "old" (solely on those grounds) in opposition to the validly established liturgy of the Church, one would run the risk of stumbling into the pit that even a so learned and heroic figure as Tertullian was unable to avoid, setting a Church "of the Spirit" in opposition to the Church represented by "a bunch of bishops."

On the contrary, a renewed appreciation of the sources of liturgy, and a familiarity with it in its "youth," should lead us to a more profound love for the Mass and the Eucharist as celebrated by the Church, and a surer grasp of the way in which they must be the foundation of the "new evangelization" to which Pope John Paul II called the people of God. Mike Aquilina is to be congratulated for making these texts accessible to a new and wide-ranging audience, allowing us to echo the cry voiced by the martyrs of North Africa in the third century: "We cannot live without the Mass!"

— FATHER JOSEPH LINCK
ST. VINCENT SEMINARY
FEAST OF ST. LAWRENCE, 2000

Introduction

The Church, in official documents, often speaks of its "living Tradition." To non-Catholics, that seems an oxymoron. "Tradition," for them, is practically defined by that which is "non-living" — fragments from a long-ago past, dusty scraps of parchment that might be interesting as museum pieces but are not particularly relevant to the Church today. They will sometimes say that the Church should receive its life from the Spirit, and not from historical relics.

They're half-right. The Church does receive its life from the Spirit, but the Spirit's movement through time is the very stuff of Tradition. The Spirit gives life to Tradition and makes it living Tradition. To deny the value of Tradition betrays a woeful misunderstanding of the Holy Spirit.

St. Augustine taught that the Holy Spirit is the soul of the Mystical Body of Christ, which is the Church. That's a beautiful expression, and most people who read the Bible will recognize that it merely draws out what is implicit in St. Paul's letters. Yet if we want to understand what Sts. Paul and Augustine are saying, we need to examine their terms. What, for example, did they mean by the soul?

The soul is what gives life to the body. When soul and body separate, death follows; the body becomes a corpse. St. Augustine taught, moreover, that the soul, created in the image of the Trinity, possesses three faculties: memory, intellect, and will — and the "father" of that "trinity" is memory.

Yet memory is underrated today. Ironically, it's almost forgotten.

Memory is what tells us who we are. Without memory, I could not complete this sentence, nor could you read it. Without memory, I could not know who I am from one moment to the next. I believe that memory may be what modern psychologists and philosophers are groping toward when they speak of "identity" or "self-consciousness."

The soul of the Church also possesses this faculty. The Church has a memory, and it's called the liturgy. The liturgy is the memory of the Church.

The Mass is the place where Tradition lives. This was its purpose from the very beginning, when Jesus commanded his apostles to "Do this in memory of me." In the Old Testament, too, the one commandment that concerns the liturgy is "Remember the Sabbath day, and keep it holy."

We must be careful not to mistake what these commands mean by remembrance. God is not urging us to keep alive a warm nostalgia for the good old days. In the Mass, God remembers his covenant and calls us to do the same. This doesn't mean we, or he, will forget the covenant at all other times. But here we commemorate, we celebrate, and we preserve our identity from moment to moment.

We "do this" in the Mass. The Mass is, for example, where the early Church kept the Scriptures. Indeed, the books we know as the New Testament were canonized not so much for devotional reading — which was rare in those days before the printing press — but for proclamation in the Mass. The controversy over which books should be included in the Bible was, to a certain extent, a running argument over which books could be read during the Mass. For, as St. Justin Martyr said in 155 A.D., one of the principal parts of the Mass was the reading of the "memoirs" of the apostles.

When the Church reads those memories aloud, Christians share in the events, the "mysteries," of the life of Christ

— again, not in a nostalgic way, but in a real and substantial way. For the Mass is a re-presentation of the passion of Christ on Calvary and a sharing in his glory in heaven. In the Mass, Christians are caught up in the one sacrifice, which is eternal.

What makes Tradition "living" is the Spirit's indwelling presence in the Church, and it is in the Mass that Christians worship "in the Spirit on the Lord's day" (Rev 1:10). In the Mass, the Church is most alive because, there, the body and soul are truly one. In the Mass, the Church knows its identity and teaches more surely than in the most solemn of papal documents. Pope Pius XI declared that the liturgy is the primary organ of the ordinary magisterium of the Church.

You will sense, in the pages of this book, the unity of the Church's identity, the unity of the Church's memory. You will see and hear the Mass as it was celebrated in the time of the apostles and in each of almost ten generations afterward. As a Catholic, you will know this Church as your Church, this Mass as your Mass. The great theologian Cardinal Yves Congar wrote in his book *Tradition and Traditions*: "We need only step into an old church, taking holy water, as Pascal and Sarapion did before us, in order to follow a Mass which has scarcely changed, even in externals." Ritual, he went on, is our "means of communication and of victory over devouring time" and "a powerful means for communion in the same reality between men separated by centuries of change and affected by very different influences."

That's what this book by Mike Aquilina is all about.

The Mass we know on Sunday — the Mass you encounter in this book — is where Tradition lives, where the Church's memory reigns "in the Spirit." The Mass enables us to remember our past, but also to remember our future. For the Mass is pointed to eternity, where past and future converge.

Read this book, then, and remember.

— SCOTT HAHN, FRANCISCAN UNIVERSITY OF STEUBENVILLE

PART I

How the Mass Began

CHAPTER 1

The Breaking of the Bread and the Prayers

How did the first Christians experience the Mass? The answer is, in some respects, very simple. We need only skim the *Catechism of the Catholic Church*, which speaks of "The Mass of all ages" (nn. 1345-1347). The first Christians, like today's Christians, experienced the Mass as a sacrament, a sacrifice, the new Passover, the re-presentation of the Paschal Mystery, the communion of God with man, the revelation of heavenly worship, and the source and summit of the Church's life and unity. Indeed, in presenting these aspects of eucharistic doctrine, the Catechism relies principally upon sources from the period covered by this book: the New Testament, the *Didache*, Irenaeus, Justin Martyr, and Hippolytus. For the Mass has an essential unity; and, though external forms have changed from age to age, the "Mass of all ages" remains the same, recognizable in the Church's doctrine and in the small details of the ritual.

Yet we need not rely exclusively on the *Catechism*. We can take the early Christians at their word. We know, generally, what they said and did when they went to Mass, and we know the Faith they believed when they drew near to the altar. They left behind just enough of a documentary trail for us to glimpse the Mass as they saw it, and to hear it as they heard it. The Mass was, after all, the act that defined them as Christians. Consider Luke's description of the Church in the days immediately following the descent of the Holy Spirit at Pentecost:

"They devoted themselves to the apostles' teaching and fellowship, to the breaking of bread and the prayers" (Acts 2:42).

So it was in the newborn Church, and so it would continue in every generation afterward. The Church took its identity from its unity in belief and charity, which was sustained by the Eucharist. The historical record is clear about this: Wherever Christianity spread, the Church immediately established the liturgy — "the breaking of the bread and the prayers" — on the "Lord's day" (Rev 1:10), which was Sunday. Indeed, every generation of the Church's history has left us evidence of its eucharistic life.

Some twenty years after Pentecost, Paul gave the Church of Corinth detailed instructions about how to conduct the Mass and how to understand it (see 1 Cor 10-11). From the next generation, the Church of Antioch in Syria left us the *Didache*, a manual that contains liturgical prayers that are still in use today. As the century turned, Pope Clement quoted from the Roman liturgy — "Holy, holy, holy Lord, God of power and might!" — in his own letter to the Corinthians. Ignatius of Antioch, in 107, wrote to the Christians of Asia Minor, setting forth the Church's eucharistic teaching in clear and forceful terms: "confess[ing] the Eucharist to be the flesh of our Savior Jesus Christ" (*Smyrnaeans* 7). Around 112, a pagan governor in the provinces, Pliny the Younger, sent Emperor Trajan a report describing how Christian worship included "food of an ordinary and innocent kind." At the middle of the second century, Justin Martyr recorded a remarkably detailed description of the Mass as it was celebrated in Rome.

The historical testimony continues unbroken from that time onward. We find it in the surviving fragments of ancient Mass prayers. We find it in Church laws that guided the work of the clergy. Sometimes we catch a passing reference to the Mass in one bishop's letter to another. The pagans, for their part, speculated about what went on behind the closed doors of the Christian rituals, and they, too, left us their peculiar witness. By the end of the third century, the Church's greatest minds and souls had begun to articulate a theology of the Eucharist. Meanwhile, heretical cults left the Church but sought to continue some form of eucharistic worship, and their odd liturgies left a trail of their own.

In all these testimonies — which make up the bulk of this book — we will catch our glimpses of the Mass as it was from the first Christian Pentecost to the generation of the Council of Nicea (the mid-fourth century). In Part I, we will examine the historical and cultural contexts of the ancient Church, as well as some of the early theological developments related to the doctrine of the Eucharist. The heart of this book, though, is Part II, which presents the actual documentary witnesses from the early Church — its members, its teachers, its wayward children, and its enemies. At the end of the second section I include, as a sort of coda, several excerpts of the mystagogical sermons of Cyril of Jerusalem, even though they belong to the generation after Nicea — just outside the proper limits of this book. Why include Cyril? Because he was reflecting on the liturgy he had received from previous generations, and because he spoke expansively, with a freedom his Christian ancestors had never known. He shows us plainly what the preceding generations could only suggest. I cite only Cyril because to include all the eucharistic witnesses of his lifetime — Athanasius, Ephrem, Aphrahat, Hilary, Ambrose, Jerome, Basil, Gregory of Nyssa, and Gregory Nazianzen — would double my page count. The book concludes instead with a brief Part III, drawing together our impressions from the early liturgy into a single narrative.

The Mass Was Everywhere

Christianity spread rapidly through the Roman Empire. One modern sociologist estimates that, in the centuries that concern us here, the Church grew at a rate of forty percent per decade. By the middle of the fourth century, there were thirty-three million Christians in an empire of sixty million people (Stark 1997:6f). That meant that the Mass was everywhere. Indeed the ubiquity of the Mass was a favorite theme of the earliest Church Fathers. Justin commented that by his day (c. 150), "There is not one single race of men . . . among whom prayers and Eucharist are not offered through the name of the crucified Jesus" (*Dialogue* 41). The Fathers commonly applied the Old Testament prophecy of Malachi to the Mass: "From the rising of the sun to its setting my name is great among the nations, and in every place incense is offered to my name, and a pure offering" (Mal 1:11). Sunrise to sunset suggested not only always, because the Mass was offered perpetually upon the earth, but also everywhere, because the Church had spread to the eastern and western horizons of the empire.

Of course, the early Christians did not call it "the Mass." *Mass* is a medieval English coinage derived from the Latin rite's words of dismissal: *Ite, missa est* ("Go, it is ended"). The Latin word *Missa*, however, appears quite early in Christian literature as a synonym for the eucharistic rites. Ambrose of Milan used it casually in a letter to his sister Marcellina, at Easter in A.D. 386. In the midst of riots and the arrival of imperial soldiers, Ambrose reported, "I kept to my duty and began to say Mass" [*missam facere cœpi*].

The majority of Christians in the first generations were Greek-speakers, and they called their worship by many names, each evocative and some even poetic. In the beginning, it was most commonly referred to as "the breaking of the bread." This, however, was immediately supplemented by "the sacrifice," and related terms such as "the offering" and "the oblation"; for the Mass was understood to be the Church's participation in the once-for-all sacrifice of the new covenant. Some called the new rite "the liturgy," from the Greek *leitourgia,* meaning "public service." From an early date, the Latins used the term "sacrament," while Greeks favored "the mysteries." Some terms were merely descriptive, such as "the table of the Lord," "the Lord's supper," "the chalice," and "the altar." Others were compact, but rich in meaning: "the passion of the Lord," "the presence," "the communion." Overwhelmingly, though, the title that won the day was "the Eucharist," from the Greek *eucharistia,* which means, literally, "thanksgiving." "Giving thanks" was, after all, the preferred term of the Gospels of Mark (14:23), Matthew (26:27), and Luke (22:17), as well the account of Paul (1 Cor 11:24).

The differences in terms reflect differences in language, culture, and even the personalities of individual writers. Yet the accounts of the early Mass show that the theology and, to a remarkable extent, the practice of the Mass were essentially the same in lands as different from one another as Persia (modern Iran) and Gaul (modern France). As the Gospel spread from place to place, the converted people found new and local ways of expressing worship, though always within the form that remained constant in Christian tradition.

We see the care with which ritual form was passed from culture to culture when we read the first letter of Paul (who was a Jew) to the Corinthians (who were Greeks): "For I received from the Lord what I also delivered to you, that the Lord Jesus on the night when he was betrayed took bread, and when he had given thanks, he broke it, and said, 'This is my body which is for you. Do this in remembrance of me.' In the same way also the cup, after supper, saying, 'This cup is the new covenant in my blood. Do this, as often as you drink it, in remembrance of me'" (1 Cor 11:23-25).

That passage from Paul shows not only the care of the early Christians for the liturgy but also the reason for their care. They celebrated the Mass because the Lord Jesus had commanded them to do so, in a most solemn way, at the decisive moment in his earthly life. Twice in Paul's account of the Last Supper, Jesus instructs his apostles to "do this," once as he takes the bread and declares it to be his body, and again as he takes the cup and declares it to contain his blood. Moreover, Paul emphasizes that this action will be at the center of the new order he is establishing with his death and resurrection. The cup "is the new covenant in my blood." Thus, the apostles, and subsequent generations, would meticulously preserve the Lord's words and actions as something precious and even divine.

Holy Orders

With ritual form came a particular communal form. For who would offer the Church's sacrifice? Ultimately, Christ made the offering as heavenly high priest (see Heb 4:14), but on earth he made it through his priestly people (see 1 Pet 2:9), his Mystical Body, the Church. The Church called certain men, however, to preside over the assembly in the place of Christ. In the New Testament (see Acts 20:17, 28; Phil 1:1; Tit 1:5-9), these men are called "bishops" (in Greek, *episkopoi*, literally "overseers"). In the early Church, it was the local bishop who ordinarily presided over the Mass.

The bishop was usually accompanied, however, by his priests (*presbuteroi*, literally "elders") and deacons (*diakonoi*, "servants"). These orders of ministry also originate in the New Testament Church (see, for example, Acts 14:23, 1 Pet 5:1, and Rev 4:4 for *presbuteroi*, Acts 6:1-6 for *diakonoi*). When the inspired authors speak of Christian ministry, they use the terminology of the sacrificial priesthood of the Jerusalem temple.

In Romans 15:16, Paul speaks, for example, of his own *hiero-urgein* (priestly ministry) and *prosphoron* (sacrificial offering).

Early Christian authors saw the Christian clergy as a true fulfillment of the priesthood first established in the Law of Moses — the orders of bishop, priest, and deacon corresponding to the ancient offices of high priest, priest, and Levite. These biblical correspondences appear as early as the first-century letter of Clement of Rome, and they are worked out theologically in the third-century *Didascalia Apostolorum*. The second-century Jewish-Christian historian Hegesippus noted that the apostles made their priestly inheritance explicit by adopting the dress and customs of the Jerusalem high priest (see Eusebius, *Church History* 5.24.3).

The three orders of Christian clergy passed with the gospel into the gentile world. The letters of Ignatius describe a Eucharist at which the bishop is flanked by his priests, as the elders flank the throne of the Almighty in the heavenly worship of the Book of Revelation: "The bishop is to preside in the place of God, while the priests are to function as the council of the apostles, and the deacons, who are most dear to me, are entrusted with the service of Jesus Christ" (*Magnesians* 6.1).

As the Church grew, this arrangement likely became impractical for worship, and Ignatius testifies that, by the beginning of the second century, the bishop could delegate the presidency over the Eucharist to his priests (see *Smyrnaeans* 8.1).

The deacons, too, played important roles in the liturgy. Depending on the geographic region, they might serve as guards at the door (an important role during persecution) and heralds of the bishop; they might lead the congregation in prayer and song, proclaim the readings, and even preach a homily; they might prepare the altar for the sacrifice and dispense the chalice of the Blood of Christ. Deacons ordinarily took the sacrament as *viaticum* ("wayfarer's food") to the sick and homebound.

To carry out Christ's command to "do this . . . in remembrance of me," the clergy was necessary, and the three orders were established in the first generation of the New Testament Church. In the generations immediately following, the roles of each "order" of clergy became clear and distinct. Yet those first congregations never lost sight of their own priestly dignity as members of Jesus Christ (see Rev 1:5-6), sharing in his eternal priesthood, or of the Eucharist as the offering of the whole Church, the priestly people of God (Jungmann 1959:16f).

CHAPTER 2

The Altar of Israel

B ut what was "this" that Jesus had commanded his apostles to "do" in his remembrance? To understand his action — and the action of the Mass — requires some knowledge of the worship of the Jews in Jesus' time. For the early Christians believed Jesus' Last Supper — and, in turn, the Mass — to be the culmination of all the worship of ancient Israel.

Jesus was a Jew, and his apostles were Jews. They conducted their lives and worship according to the patterns established in the law and tradition of Israel. From childhood, Jesus made regular pilgrimages to the holy city, Jerusalem, for the holy days. There, he worshiped at the Temple, participating in the sacrifices offered by the people through the priests. He knew that near the heart of the Temple was kept the "bread of the presence," or "showbread" (see Ex 25:29, Lev 24:9). Weekly, or perhaps more often, he attended a synagogue, the houses where rabbis proclaimed and taught from the law and the prophets, and where the congregation prayed from the psalms and other ritual prayers.

Jesus probably also held a weekly solemn "fellowship meal" (*chaburah*) with his disciples. On the eve of the Sabbath, families or groups of friends traditionally conducted such a meal, which began with the blessing of bread and wine (Dix 1945:50ff; Pierse 1909:163ff). These meals, conducted in the home, were somewhat formal events with standard ritual washings and prayers (*berakoth*): "Blessed are you, O Lord our God, king of the universe, creator of the fruit of the vine. . . . Blessed are you, O Lord our God, king of the universe, who brings forth bread from the earth."

A form of sacrifice with which Jesus was surely familiar was the *todah*, or "thanksgiving." The *todah* was an offering of praise in gratitude for deliverance from some dire circumstance (Ratzinger 1986:51ff). Many of the psalms record standard *todah* prayers (see, for example, Psalms 22 and 116). Along with the prayer, the person who had received deliverance was to offer a sacrificial meal of bread and wine, shared with his friends. The Talmud records the rabbinic teaching that, with the coming of Israel's anointed deliverer, the Messiah, "all sacrifices will cease except the *todah* sacrifice. This will never cease in all eternity" (quoted in Hahn 1999:33).

For some Jews of Jesus' day, the bread and wine perpetually offered for praise and thanksgiving were the very image of the awaited kingdom of God on earth. We find a record of such hope in the Dead Sea Scrolls:

> And when they shall gather for the common table, to eat and to drink new wine . . . let no man extend his hand over the first-fruits of bread and wine before the priest; for it is he who shall bless the first-fruits of bread and wine, and shall be the first to extend his hand over the bread. Thereafter, the Messiah of Israel shall extend his hand over the bread, and all the congregation of the community shall utter a blessing, each man in the order of his dignity (Vermes 1975:121; see also Danielou 1958:25ff).

The *chaburah, berakoth*, and *todah* were important elements of Jesus' religious culture. However, he uttered his command to "do this" in the context of the Passover meal, the *seder*. The Passover, the single most important event of the Jewish year, commemorated God's deliverance of Israel from slavery in Egypt. At the Passover meal, every Jewish family renewed its covenant with the God of Israel.

The *seder* was a tightly scripted household event with pre-scribed roles for different family members. The family recalled — through readings and prayers — the events of the Exodus: the smearing of lamb's blood on the doorposts; the hasty meal of lamb and unleavened bread; the angel's slaughter of the firstborn in every Egyptian household; and Israel's flight through the Red Sea. In the course of the meal, the father of the family pronounced a blessing over unleavened bread and four cups of wine. The ritual meal ended with the singing of the Hallel Psalms (Ps 112-117 and 135), which are songs of praise.

All of these details of the *seder* correspond closely with the Gospel narratives of the Last Supper in Matthew, Mark, and Luke, as well as Paul's account in his First Letter to the Corinthians (Zeitlin 1989:xi-xv). John's Gospel presents a different but complementary account of the events of that particular Passover meal (Pixner 221ff; Cavaletti 1990:23).

The Last Supper was the first of the events that marked the culmination of Jesus' saving work. From that *seder*, he proceeded to his trial and death, then to his resurrection and glorification. The events would be forever stamped with the character of Passover. The Church calls them, collectively, the Paschal Mystery — from *Pesach*, the Hebrew word for Passover.

Continuity and Communion

In Luke's Gospel, Jesus describes himself as impelled toward his last *seder* with his apostles: "I have earnestly desired to eat this passover with you before I suffer; for I tell you that I shall not eat it until it is fulfilled in the kingdom of God" (Lk 22:15). Jesus conveys a clear sense of urgency about what he is going to accomplish.

Luke continues with the New Testament's fullest account of the institution of the Eucharist, repeating almost verbatim the words Paul wrote to the Corinthians:

> And he took bread, and when he had given thanks he broke it and gave it to them, saying, "This is my body which is given for you. Do this in remembrance of me." And likewise the cup after supper, saying, "This cup which is poured out for you is the new covenant in my blood."
>
> —Lk 22:19-20

These are the words that set this *seder* apart from any other. Jesus took the unleavened bread and, blessing it, pronounced that it was his body; he took the cup of wine and, blessing it, pronounced that it was his blood. Then he told his apostles to perform the same action in memory of him. The *todah*, the *chaburah*, and the *seder* had all included blessings of bread and wine, but never had anyone made such a claim for the efficacy of the prayers of blessing, that they should become the flesh and blood of God-made-man.

After the supper, Jesus and the apostles sang the Hallel Psalms (see Mt 26:30), and he went out to give up his body and shed his blood.

Yet his sense of urgency, his earnest desire, remained. For, on the day he rose from the dead, he wasted no time before repeating the action of the Last Supper. Encountering two disciples on the road to Emmaus, he prevented them from recognizing him. Only when they sat at table were their eyes opened, and they knew him "in the breaking of the bread" (Lk 24:35).

For the first Christians, most of whom were Jews, the Eucharist of Jesus Christ was inseparable from the mystery of the Passover. Paul states that Christ is now "our paschal lamb" (1 Cor 5:7); he is, therefore, the sacrifice and the price of redemption, as the lamb was for the firstborn sons of Israel at the Exodus. Paul goes on: "Let us, therefore, celebrate the festival, not with the old leaven . . . but with the unleavened bread of sincerity and truth" (1 Cor 5:8).

All the worship of ancient Israel — the sacrifices, the assemblies, the commemorations, the blessings, and the prayers — had led God's people to this moment. When the first Christians knew him "in the breaking of the bread," they saw that all the rites they had known before were now fulfilled, transformed, and glorified. This celebration of the Eucharist, which Christ had commanded them to "do" in his memory, was clearly continuous with the liturgy of Israel. Yet it was also something strikingly new — a new covenant in his blood.

Nonetheless, the disciples still belonged to Israel; for Israel, too, had been fulfilled, transformed, and glorified in the Church. The first Christians continued to think of themselves as Jews. As one scholar wrote: "There was never any brutal rupture between the Church and the Mosaic religion" (Cabrol 1934:ch.1). Put positively: "Early Christianity . . . was rooted in the native soil of Palestine" (Wise et al. 1996:34).

The continuity is clear in the pages of the New Testament. Believers in Jerusalem attended the Temple daily (see Acts 2:46; 3:1). The apostles found many opportunities to preach in synagogues (see Acts 13:13ff; 14:1; 16:1, 10, 16; 17:2-3; 18:4, 19; 19:8). The "breaking of the bread," like the *chaburah* and Passover meal, remained a domestic ritual (see Acts 2:46). The *Letter of James* (2:2) continues to use the Greek word *synagogos* for the Christian assembly. Indeed, recent archeological excavations show that Christian and rabbinic synagogues coexisted across the street from one another in Capernaum; that the Christians maintained a synagogue on Mount Zion in Jerusalem (the site of the Last Supper); and that Christians and Jews shared burial grounds till late in the third century (Stark 1997:68f; Pixner 1997:212). Some local Churches, especially in the East, continued to observe the Jewish Sabbath (along with the Lord's day on Sunday) for centuries.

With the Roman destruction of the Jerusalem Temple in the year 70, relations between Christians and other Jews became more complicated. Whereas the Jews in Judea had tolerated a widely diverse range of religious expression, in the dispersion the piety of the Pharisees prevailed. According to some accounts, at a council held in Jamnia in 100, the rabbis decreed that "the Nazarenes" (the followers of Jesus) should be excommunicated from the synagogues and cursed in the synagogue service. Still, many scholars (including Bouyer the liturgist and Stark the sociologist) believe that the excommunication was applied only erratically, and that Christians and Jews enjoyed some degree of mutual influence well into the fifth century.

CHAPTER 3

All Things Made New

Christian worship was modeled after — or, rather, continuous with — the worship of Israel. Many prayers and songs of the synagogue, Temple, and the Jewish home remain in the Christian liturgy even into modern times. The Sanctus, or "Holy, holy, holy," for example, is based on Isaiah 6:3, which was the starting point of the *Kedushah*, used in the synagogue service every Sabbath. The Sanctus appears early in Christian literature, including the Book of Revelation (4:8), and afterward in the works of Clement of Rome, Tertullian in North Africa, and Origen in Egypt. Other relics of Israel's liturgies include the Alleluia, from the Hallel Psalms recited in the Passover meal, and many common refrains, such as "Blessed is he who comes in the name of the Lord!"

Some scholars believe that the first Christian liturgies were, quite simply, Jewish texts with added Christological and Trinitarian language (Bouyer 1968). Sofia Cavaletti observes that the synagogue service closely parallels the early Christian Liturgy of the Word, roughly the first half of the Mass, while the sequence of prayers in the Jewish Passover meal closely corresponds to the order of the earliest eucharistic prayers (1990:15ff).

Still, we have no clear and certain record of *how* the first Christians conducted their liturgies. From Scripture and the earliest records, we know that Christians celebrated an *agape*, or "love feast," in addition to the Eucharist. At this feast, they shared a more complete meal. We know that in the beginning — in Corinth at least — the *agape* was celebrated in conjunction with the Eucharist (see 1 Cor 11). It is possible that this arrangement was a peculiarity of the Church in Corinth. It is also possible that the context of a full meal is a direct inheritance from the Jewish *chaburah*, but that the idea of a solemn feast did not translate well into other cultures, thus bringing on Paul's censure of the Corinthians' behavior (see also Jude 11). Perhaps for this reason, the *agape* was separated from the Eucharist very early on, probably by the end of the first century, though the Church continued to celebrate its love feasts well into the third century.

This separation may also explain why some ancient writers, such as Pliny, speak of two Christian meetings on Sunday. The Church could have met once for Mass and once for a common feast. Some scholars, however, hold that the two separate meetings were for the morning proclamation of the word (to which anyone, baptized or not, could be invited) and the evening celebration of the Eucharist (which was for believers only). The apostolic Church did, after all, attend the synagogue readings, but reserved the "breaking of the bread" for the Christian home.

Another theory places the Liturgy of the Word on the Sabbath, like the synagogue service, and the Liturgy of the Eucharist on Sunday. Such a separation could not have lasted long, however, as many early sources testify to the liturgical unity of word and sacrament.

The Heavenly Liturgy
Yet, while the Mass had its roots in the worship of Israel, Christ had clearly established it as something "new." According to Cavaletti, the essential difference between Christian

and Jewish liturgies was that, "whereas in the synagogue salvation is hoped for, in the Church it is announced as already accomplished" (ibid. 7).

Indeed, for the early Christians, the Mass was the source of life itself, and life was unthinkable without it. Said a North African who faced martyrdom during the reign of Emperor Diocletian: "Without fear of any kind we have celebrated the Mass, because it cannot be missed. . . . We cannot live without the Mass." One of his fellows added: "Christians make the Mass and the Mass makes the Christians, and one cannot exist without the other" (Hamman 1967:16). They and their companions, known as the Martyrs of Abitina, were sentenced to death precisely for their refusal to renounce the Eucharist.

For Ignatius, the Eucharist was the "medicine of immortality" (*Ephesians* 20). For Irenaeus, "our bodies, when they receive the Eucharist, are no longer corruptible, but have the hope of the resurrection to eternity" (*Against Heresies* 4.18.5). Conversely, to abstain from the Eucharist — or, worse, to profane the sacrament — meant certain death. Paul warned the Corinthians: "Any one who eats and drinks without discerning the body eats and drinks judgment upon himself. That is why many of you are weak and ill, and some have died" (1 Cor 11:29-30). Ignatius and Irenaeus echoed Paul on this liability, as they echoed him on the reward.

The reward was eternal life in heaven, which explains why those North African martyrs, and many others, were willing to give up their earthly lives rather than miss the Mass. The pagan Romans, on the other hand, knew that attending Mass was, essentially, an act of treason; for Christians who bound themselves to Christ could no longer worship the emperor as a god or follow the traditional, state-sponsored religion.

At the liturgy, the Christians were easy targets for their persecutors. The Romans knew the Christians' festal day, and believers ordinarily met with their bishop in family homes. The civil authorities needed only to watch for any unusually large gathering on a Sunday — a day that had no special significance to pagans or Jews.

The Christians preferred to attend Mass not only for the promise of heaven in the future, but for the reality of heaven in the Eucharist. In the Mass, Christians already lived within the messianic age foreshadowed in the Old Testament, the *todah*, and the Dead Sea Scrolls. The Book of Revelation (especially chapters 4, 5, and 19) mystically represents the liturgy as the "marriage supper of the Lamb" — the Lamb of the new Passover, who is Jesus Christ (Hahn 1999). It is likely that many details of Revelation's heavenly liturgy are intended to reflect the earthly worship of the early Church (Quasten 1973:72; Dix 1945:28, 314; Gassner 1950:81ff; Jones 1992:201ff). As will be evident throughout the selections in this book, the early Fathers habitually associated Revelation with the Eucharist (see, for example, Irenaeus and Hippolytus). For both Irenaeus and Tertullian, the earthly altar was united with the altar of heaven. To go to Mass was to live in heaven already (Danielou 1956:128ff). The historian Jaroslav Pelikan noted that this interpretation of Christ's *parousia*, his coming, was universal in the early Church:

> The coming of Christ was "already" and "not yet" . . . he had come already in the Eucharist, and would come at the last in the new cup that he would drink with them in his Father's kingdom . . . The eucharistic liturgy was not a compensation for the postponement of the parousia, but a way of celebrating the presence of one who had promised to return (Pelikan 1971:126f; Hahn 2005:108-110).

CHAPTER 4

More Precious than Gold

For the early Christians, Mass was the meeting of heaven and earth. Nevertheless, to be in heaven-on-earth was not to live "alone" with God. From Paul and the *Didache* onward, the Christians preached the unifying power of the Eucharist within the Church community (De Lubac 1988:88). "Because there is one bread, we who are many are one body, for we all partake of the one bread" (1 Cor 10:17). "Even as this broken bread was scattered over the hills, and was gathered together and became one, so let your Church be gathered together from the ends of the earth into your kingdom" (*Didache* 9). Ignatius, in his turn, wrote: "Take care, then, to have only one Eucharist. For there is one flesh of our Lord Jesus Christ, and one cup to show forth the unity of His blood" (*Philadelphians* 4).

This close, mystical communion of the Church was probably easy for those early believers to imagine. Until the legalization of Christianity in 313, the Church could own few buildings. So, as we saw in the Acts of the Apostles, the faithful usually assembled for the Eucharist in family homes. Sometimes, when wealthy families converted, they turned over substantial estates for liturgical use. The Basilica of San Clemente in Rome may have been built upon just such a mansion. Another "house-church" has been excavated, somewhat intact, at Dura-Europus, in modern Syria.

Still, though the first Christians were "at home" with the Eucharist, their reverence was profound. In the third century, Origen wrote: "You who are accustomed to attending the divine mysteries know how, when you receive the body of the Lord, you guard it with all care and reverence lest any small part should fall from it, lest any piece of the consecrated gift be lost." In the fourth century, Cyril of Jerusalem exhorted his people to take the same care:

> Tell me, if anyone gave you grains of gold, would you not hold them with utmost care, on guard against losing any? Will you not take greater care not to lose a crumb of what is more precious than gold or jewels?

That reverence extended to the trappings of the liturgy as well — the altar, the plates, and the chalices — which were always made of the finest materials the local Church could afford. Tertullian, for example, described chalices decorated with images of Christ (*On Modesty* 7, 10). And, in 303, a Roman court in North Africa recorded the following items that had been confiscated from a house-church: two golden chalices, six silver chalices, six silver dishes, a silver bowl, seven silver lamps, two torches, seven short bronze lampstands with their lamps, and eleven bronze lamps on chains (Dix 1945:24).

In the following century, Jerome would write of the need

> . . . to instruct by the authority of Scripture ignorant people in all the churches concerning the reverence with which they must handle holy things and minister at Christ's altar; and to impress upon them that the sacred chalices, veils, and other accessories used in the celebration of the Lord's passion are not mere lifeless and

senseless objects devoid of holiness, but that rather, from their association with the body and blood of the Lord, they are to be venerated with the same awe as the body and the blood themselves (*Letter* 114.2).

Clergy were expected to give the same careful attention to the words of the liturgy. Paul emphasized the need for faithful transmission of the eucharistic tradition, for it had originated with Jesus himself: "I received from the Lord what I also delivered to you" (1 Cor 11:23). The *Didache*, Justin, and Hippolytus indicate that some Mass texts were fixed at a very early date, but these same sources also suggest that priests were permitted to add their own words to the liturgy. Prudence, however, led to increasing regulation of the Mass as time went on. While Hippolytus encouraged a bishop to pray "in his own words," he immediately added that his words should, if possible, be "grand and elevated," and in any event "orthodox" — which suggests that improvised prayers were sometimes sliding into sloppy or even heretical language (*Apostolic Tradition* 10.3-5).

In the third century, the Cappadocian Bishop Firmilian spoke of regional differences in the liturgy but also acknowledged a common core that his North African colleague, Cyprian, could recognize. In Egypt, Clement of Alexandria referred to rules, or "canons," for the proper celebration of Mass. By the middle of that century, disciplinary manuals known as "Church orders," such as the *Didascalia,* offered copious legislation concerning the liturgy. All the evidence indicates that certain prayers — such as the "Holy, Holy, Holy" and the dialogue proceeding from "Lift up your hearts" — were almost universal by the middle of the third century, though probably much earlier.

The Real Presence

This reverence and extreme care for liturgical detail followed from the Church's belief in the Real Presence of Jesus Christ in the Eucharist. Jesus had spoken of the Eucharist in the most graphic, physical terms.

> "I am the living bread which came down from heaven; if any one eats of this bread, he will live for ever; and the bread which I shall give for the life of the world is my flesh."
>
> — Jn 6:51

The early Church took him at his word and always spoke of the Eucharist with the same flesh-and-blood realism. Belief in Jesus' Real Presence was essential to a Christian's profession of faith. "For any one who eats and drinks without discerning the body," wrote Paul, "eats and drinks judgment upon himself" (1 Cor 11:29). For Ignatius, the distinguishing mark of heretics was their denial of the Real Presence:

> They abstain from the Eucharist and from prayer, because they do not confess the Eucharist to be the flesh of our Savior Jesus Christ, which suffered for our sins, and which the Father, in his goodness, raised up again.
>
> — *Smyrnaeans* 7

Justin, in turn, wrote that "the food blessed by the prayer of his word . . . is the flesh and blood of Jesus who was made flesh" (*First Apology* 66).

Christ's presence in the Eucharist was lasting, and not confined to the time of the liturgy. We see this belief in Tertullian, who explains that Christians in his place and time would carry the eucharistic bread home from Sunday Mass so that they could administer Communion to themselves throughout the week. Justin describes deacons taking Communion to the sick who were homebound. Hippolytus, rather quaintly, urges Christians to take care to reserve the Body of Christ where no mouse could nibble at it: "For it is the body of Christ . . . and not to be treated lightly."

The Church held to this understanding from the start, though its theological language developed only gradually. As with the Trinity, so with the Eucharist: The early Fathers were sometimes imprecise in their formulations, and later ages have rejected certain phrases in the works of Justin, Irenaeus, Clement of Alexandria, Tertullian, and Origen. This does not mean that these men held heretical views, but rather that they did not yet possess the language to express the doctrine. Sometimes the Church defined doctrines with precision only after they had been challenged by heretics.

Eucharistic heresies and aberrations did arise in the first Christian centuries. Ignatius wrote of those who denied the doctrine of the Real Presence. Other sects veered in practice. Several groups swore off alcohol, and so refused to consecrate a chalice of wine in the Mass. Some celebrated "bread-only Eucharists." Others consecrated a cup of water with their bread. Firmilian wrote to Cyprian of a sorceress who assumed ordination for herself and went about simulating the Mass. Irenaeus reported that a magician named Marcus claimed the priesthood for himself and worked illusions with his chalice while he recited the eucharistic prayers. Epiphanius and later Fathers claimed that some fringe cults, calling themselves Christians, used their liturgies as occasions for drunkenness, sexual license, and even murder.

Clarity and precision came with the orthodox responses to eucharistic abuses. Cyprian taught that, by removing wine from the liturgy, the heretics were taking away two things: a divinely appointed image of Christ's blood, and a symbol — in the mixed cup of wine and water — of the union of the people with Christ (*Epistle* 62). Irenaeus pointed out that the mixed cup also symbolized the union of Christ's divine and human natures (*Against Heresies* 4.100.2).

The Eucharist was, in a certain sense, the test and measure of Christian faith. Again, in the words of Irenaeus: "Our way of thinking is attuned to the Eucharist, and the Eucharist confirms our way of thinking" (*Against Heresies* 4.18.5).

CHAPTER 5

Word and Bread

A profoundly eucharistic spirituality pervaded the life of the early Christians and illumined their reading of the Bible. Indeed, the Mass was the place where Christians encountered the Scriptures. More than a millennium before the invention of the printing press, few people could afford "books," which were parchments copied out by hand — a laborious and expensive process. Moreover, few could read. Yet congregations absorbed the words of Scripture that were proclaimed during the liturgy and were explained in homilies by their bishops and priests. The liturgy was itself saturated with Scripture passages and allusions.

In both the Old and New Testaments, the faithful found intimations of the Eucharist. The narrative of the Last Supper often appears in this context, as do Jesus' Bread of Life discourse and the eleventh chapter of Paul's First Letter to the Corinthians. But these "literal" references, while foundational, were only the beginning. Like Jesus and Paul, the early Christians also discerned a "spiritual" sense of the Scriptures, a mystical or moral meaning behind the literal sense of a story or precept. Thus, while they believed that Jesus' multiplication of loaves was a true and miraculous event, they also believed he performed it as a "sign" prefiguring his Eucharist. Indeed, that connection was so commonplace in the early Church that Origen, uncharacteristically, did not bother to explain it in his commentary on Matthew (10.25), but merely mentioned it in passing.

The early Christians used the same interpretive key on the wedding feast at Cana, where Jesus changed water into wine. Likewise, when Jesus taught the Lord's Prayer, Tertullian, Cyprian, and Cyril understood the "daily bread" to be the Eucharist.

Such eucharistic interpretation extended also to the Old Testament, where the Fathers found many "types" that would be fulfilled in the "antitype" of the Mass. A *type* is the foreshadowing of something greater; Adam, for example, is a type of Christ (see Rom 5:14). An *antitype* is the fulfillment of the thing foreshadowed: Christ, then, is the antitype of Adam. Read in the context of the Eucharist, Psalm 23 with its "table" and anointing was, for Cyril of Jerusalem, a foreshadowing of the sacraments. For Origen and many others, the story of the Passover and Exodus was rich in eucharistic typology, as was the account of Melchizedek in Genesis (14). The offering of fine flour by those cured of leprosy (see Lev 14:10) was, according to Justin, a sign of the bread that would be offered for the forgiveness of sins.

Overwhelmingly, the prophecy most often applied to the Eucharist was from Malachi.

> For from the rising of the sun to its setting my name is great among the nations, and in every place incense is offered to my name, and a pure offering; for my name is great among the nations, says the Lord of hosts. But you profane it when you say that the LORD's table is polluted, and the food for it may be despised.
>
> — MAL 1:11-12

For the Fathers, the Eucharist was the Church's participation in the one sacrifice of Christ, the everlasting hope and extension of his love. In the accounts of the *Didache*, Ignatius,

Justin, Irenaeus, Cyprian, Cyril, and many others, the Mass was "*the* sacrifice" offered by the Church — the Church that was itself the Body of Christ. Christ, then, was the offering — the Passover Lamb — and Christ was the priest who made the offering. The offering was perfect, and the priest was sinless, thus fulfilling in glory (and in the Church) all the sacrifices of ancient Israel.

A Resounding Silence

Providence has permitted us some several witnesses from the first three hundred years of Christianity. It is important for us to understand, however, that these testimonies were exceptional. For the early Church's most resounding witness to the power of the Eucharist was its silence.

In almost every instance when the Fathers speak of the Eucharist, we find them urging their listeners not to repeat the doctrine to nonbelievers. Indeed, the unbaptized were forbidden to remain at the Mass beyond the Liturgy of the Word. The eucharistic prayer — in the East called the *anaphora*, and in the West the *canon* — was for baptized Christians only.

Later scholars called this tendency to reticence the "discipline of the secret." Throughout this book, you'll find it applied in varying degrees and in different ways by individual Fathers. Some would only hint at a eucharistic meaning; others would speak abstractly of the doctrines without revealing the actual words of the Mass; still others would speak plainly, then command secrecy with the direst warnings.

Why did the Church keep the best of its Good News shrouded in secrecy? The Fathers offer many explanations:

- The mysteries of faith were so great that reducing them to words would be a profanation.

- The Church should not risk exposing the mysteries to ridicule by those who would not understand.
- Unbelievers were unworthy even to hear of the mysteries, since they had not received sufficient grace through baptism.
- No one should presume upon the work of a teacher in the Church.
- The sacraments were intimate matters and, like intimacy in marriage, were not suitable subjects for public conversation.
- The best witness of eucharistic faith is not abundant words, but a pervasive culture of Christian charity. The third-century *Didascalia* put it eloquently: "Widows and orphans should be revered like the altar."

The Church's reticence makes it difficult for us, in the third millennium, to study the heart and mind of the Church in the first millennium. Yet history has not left us completely in the dark, for there is light in the texts that have come down to us. We can study them and pray with them, and we should.

Moreover, we can share in the same table they shared with Christ; for the bread is one, not just *everywhere* but *always*; and from one chalice alone has wisdom come to man, from the time of the Fathers to our own day.

Those long-ago disciples on the road to Emmaus did not know Christ when he opened the Scriptures for them — though that illumination surely took them further along the road with him. No, they knew him in the breaking of the bread. In the same way, millions would come to know Jesus in the years immediately after he ascended to heaven.

In times of persecution, there were few opportunities to encounter Christ through the public works of the Church. The empire forbade such works. Nor could passersby come to know him in the grandeur of cathedrals, since the Church owned no such property.

They knew their Lord in the breaking of the bread, and across the millennia they — and he — urge us to do the same.

PART II

The Testimony
of Witnesses

CHAPTER 6

The New Testament

The New Testament provided the foundation for all the eucharistic preaching, doctrine, and theology of the early Church. There is hardly a chapter of the Gospels that the Fathers did not relate to the Mass in some way. Jesus referred to himself as "the living bread come down from heaven," and it was bread that he blessed and called his body. This bread, then, was somehow central to his life and work — like the passion and resurrection. Indeed, the Eucharist was of a piece with the Paschal Mystery. Thus, just as the passion of Christ lies hidden in the small details of the Gospels, so does the Eucharist. The Fathers delighted to note, for example, that the Savior chose for his birthplace the town of Bethlehem, which in Hebrew means "House of Bread." (The Fathers' eucharistic interpretation of many other passages — including the Lord's Prayer and the wedding feast at Cana — appear throughout the later chapters of this book.)

The normal time when Christians "received" the Gospel was during the Mass. Thus, parts of the New Testament were likely written with that liturgical context in mind — and, so, often prove inscrutable apart from that context. The Book of Revelation and the Letter to the Hebrews can seem almost surreal to those who are ignorant of their recurring liturgical themes and imagery — priests, altar, sacrifice, incense, hymns, and heavenly worship.

Several New Testament passages, however, stand out for their overtly eucharistic character: the accounts of the Last Supper in Matthew, Mark, and Luke; the Bread of Life discourse, with the accompanying multiplication of the loaves, in John; the accounts of the "breaking of the bread" in the Acts of the Apostles; the advice on worship in Paul's First Letter to the Corinthians; and the descriptions of the heavenly liturgy in Hebrews and Revelation. Certain phrases recur, from the Last Supper to the liturgies of the apostles: The action is the "breaking of the bread" and the giving of thanks (in Greek, *eucharistein*).

The passages below are from the Revised Standard Version, Catholic Edition, of the Holy Bible.

Luke: The Last Supper

Luke's Gospel provides the most detailed account of the institution of the Eucharist at the Last Supper. (Parallel passages appear in Matthew 26:27-29 and Mark 14:22-25.) The drama continues on the day of Jesus' resurrection, as he breaks bread with two disciples, who immediately recognize his presence.

And when the hour came, he sat at table, and the apostles with him. And he said to them, "I have earnestly desired to eat this passover with you before I suffer; for I tell you I shall not eat it until it is fulfilled in the kingdom of God." And he took a cup, and when he had given thanks he said, "Take this, and divide it among yourselves; for I tell you that from now on I shall not drink of the fruit of the vine until the kingdom of God comes." And he took bread, and when he had given thanks he broke it and gave it to them, saying, "This is my body which is given for you. Do this in remembrance of me." And likewise the cup after supper, saying, "This cup which is poured out for you is the new covenant in my blood."

— Lk 22:14-20

Luke: The Road to Emmaus

Unaware that their traveling companion is the risen Jesus, two disciples confess their despondence over their Master's death. Tracing the course of the Mass, Jesus opens the Scriptures for them and gives them his Real Presence in the "breaking of the bread."

And he said to them, "O foolish men, and slow of heart to believe all that the prophets have spoken! Was it not necessary that the Christ should suffer these things and enter into his glory?" And beginning with Moses and all the prophets, he interpreted to them in all the scriptures the things concerning himself.

So they drew near to the village to which they were going. He appeared to be going further, but they constrained him, saying, "Stay with us, for it is toward evening and the day is now far spent." So he went in to stay with them. When he was at table with them, he took the bread and blessed, and broke it, and gave it to them. And their eyes were opened and they recognized him; and he vanished out of their sight. They said to each other, "Did not our hearts burn within us while he talked to us on the road, while he opened to us the scriptures?" And they rose that same hour and returned to Jerusalem; and they found the eleven gathered together and those who were with them, who said, "The Lord has risen indeed, and has appeared to Simon!" Then they told what had happened on the road, and how he was known to them in the breaking of the bread.

— Lk 24:25-35

John: The Bread of Life

The sequence of events in the sixth chapter of John's Gospel moves from Jesus' miraculous multiplication of loaves to his long discourse on the bread of life, which he revealed to be his flesh. All this took place, John tells us, just before Passover. Thus, the readings in the synagogue would have focused on the miraculous events of Israel's exodus from Egypt, including the appearance of manna from heaven (Num 11). By his own miracle and by the words of his sermon, Jesus demonstrates that the ancient manna, the bread that fell miraculously from heaven to feed the Israelites, prefigured the greater miracle of the Eucharist, the heavenly bread that will feed the Church. As the discourse proceeds and the Jews challenge Jesus, his imagery becomes increasingly precise and graphically realistic. From the beginning, in the account of the multiplication, eucharistic language abounds: "He had given thanks."

Jesus went to the other side of the Sea of Galilee, which is the Sea of Tiberias. And a multitude followed him, because they saw the signs which he did on those who were diseased. Jesus went up on the mountain, and there sat down with his disciples. Now the Passover, the feast of the Jews, was at hand. Lifting up his eyes, then, and seeing that a multitude was coming to him, Jesus said to Philip, "How are we to buy bread, so that these people may eat?" This he said to test him, for he himself knew what he would do. Philip answered him, "Two hundred denarii would not buy enough bread for each of them to get a little." One of his disciples, Andrew, Simon Peter's brother, said to him, "There is a lad here who has five barley loaves and two fish; but what are they among so many?" Jesus said, "Make the people sit down." Now there was much grass in the place; so the men sat down, in number about five thousand. Jesus then took the loaves, and when he had given thanks, he distributed them to those who were seated; so also the fish, as much as they wanted. And when they had eaten their fill, he told his disciples, "Gather up the fragments left over, that nothing may be lost." So they gathered them up and filled twelve baskets with fragments from the five barley loaves, left by those who had eaten. When the people saw the sign which he had done, they said, "This is indeed the prophet who is to come into the world!" . . .

On the next day the people . . . found him on the other side of the sea, [and] they said to him, "Rabbi, when did you come here?" Jesus answered them, "Truly, truly, I say to you, you seek me, not because you saw signs, but because you ate your fill of the loaves. Do not labor for the food which perishes, but for the food which endures to eternal life, which the Son of man will give to you; for on him has God the Father set his seal." Then they said to him, "What must we do, to be doing the works of God?" Jesus answered them, "This is the work of God, that you believe in him whom he has sent." So they said to him, "Then what sign do you do, that we may see, and believe you? What work do you perform? Our fathers ate the manna in the wilderness; as it is written, 'He gave them bread from heaven to eat.' " Jesus then said to them,

"Truly, truly, I say to you, it was not Moses who gave you the bread from heaven; my Father gives you the true bread from heaven. For the bread of God is that which comes down from heaven, and gives life to the world." They said to him, "Lord, give us this bread always."

Jesus said to them, "I am the bread of life; he who comes to me shall not hunger, and he who believes in me shall never thirst. But I said to you that you have seen me and yet do not believe. All that the Father gives me will come to me; and him who comes to me I will not cast out. For I have come down from heaven, not to do my own will, but the will of him who sent me; and this is the will of him who sent me, that I should lose nothing of all that he has given me, but raise it up at the last day. For this is the will of my Father, that every one who sees the Son and believes in him should have eternal life; and I will raise him up at the last day."

The Jews then murmured at him, because he said, "I am the bread which came down from heaven." They said, "Is not this Jesus, the son of Joseph, whose father and mother we know? How does he now say, 'I have come down from heaven'?" Jesus answered them, "Do not murmur among yourselves. No one can come to me unless the Father who sent me draws him; and I will raise him up at the last day. It is written in the prophets, 'And they shall all be taught by God.' Every one who has heard and learned from the Father comes to me. Not that any one has seen the Father except him who is from God; he has seen the Father. Truly, truly, I say to you, he who believes has eternal life. I am the bread of life. Your fathers ate the manna in the wilderness, and they died. This is the bread which comes down from heaven, that a man may eat of it and not die. I am the living bread which came down from heaven; if any one eats of this bread, he will live for ever; and the bread which I shall give for the life of the world is my flesh."

The Jews then disputed among themselves, saying, "How can this man give us his flesh to eat?" So Jesus said to them, "Truly, truly, I say to you, unless you eat the flesh of the Son of man and drink his blood, you have no life in you; he who eats my flesh and drinks my blood has eternal life, and I will raise him up at the last day. For my flesh is food indeed, and my blood is drink indeed. He who eats my flesh and drinks my blood abides in me, and I in him. As the living Father sent me, and I live because of the Father, so he who eats me will live because of me. This is the bread which came down from heaven, not such as the fathers ate and died; he who eats this bread will live for ever." This he said in the synagogue, as he taught at Capernaum.

Many of his disciples, when they heard it, said, "This is a hard saying; who can listen to it?" But Jesus, knowing in himself that his disciples murmured at it, said to them, "Do you take offense at this? Then what if you were to see the Son of man ascending where he was before? It is the spirit that gives life, the flesh is of no avail; the words that I have spoken to you are spirit and life. But there are some of you that do not believe." For Jesus knew from the first who those were that did not believe, and who it was that would betray him. And he said, "This is why I told you that no one can come to me unless it is granted him by the Father."

After this many of his disciples drew back and no longer went about with him. Jesus said to the twelve, "Do you also wish to go away?" Simon Peter answered him, "Lord, to whom shall we go? You have the words of eternal life; and we have believed, and have come to know, that you are the Holy One of God."

— Jn 6:1-14, 22, 25-69

Paul: The Eucharist at Corinth

Corinth was a prosperous port city whose fractious citizens were given to excesses in bodily and spiritual indulgence. Paul expresses horror at what he hears about their agape-Eucharists, where some get drunk and glutted while others go hungry. These actions have dire consequences — sickness and death to the offenders. The abuses at Corinth might explain why the agape was separated from the Eucharist very early in the Church's history. Paul's account of the Last Supper was likely the first to be set in writing; it corresponds closely to that of Luke, who was Paul's disciple. Note, too, the recurring images of Israel's exodus and Passover, and the contrast of pagan sacrifice with the Christian sacrifice of the Mass.

I want you to know, brethren, that our fathers were all under the cloud, and all passed through the sea, and all were baptized into Moses in the cloud and in the sea, and all ate the same supernatural food and all drank the same supernatural drink. For they drank from the supernatural Rock which followed them, and the Rock was Christ. Nevertheless with most of them God was not pleased; for they were overthrown in the wilderness.

Now these things are warnings for us, not to desire evil as they did. Do not be idolaters as some of them were; as it is written, "The people sat down to eat and drink and rose up to dance." We must not indulge in immorality as some of them did, and twenty-three thousand fell in a single day. We must not put the Lord to the test, as some of them did and were destroyed by serpents; nor grumble, as some of them did and were destroyed by the Destroyer. Now these things happened to them as a warning, but they were written down for our instruction, upon whom the end of the ages has come. Therefore let any one who thinks that he stands take heed lest he fall. No temptation has overtaken you that is not common to man. God is faithful, and he will not let you be tempted beyond your strength, but with the temptation will also provide the way of escape, that you may be able to endure it.

Therefore, my beloved, shun the worship of idols. I speak as to sensible men; judge for yourselves what I say. The cup of blessing which we bless, is it not a participation in the blood of Christ? The bread which we break, is it not a participation in the body of Christ? Because there is one bread, we who are many are one body, for we all partake of the one bread. Consider the people of Israel; are not those who eat the sacrifices partners in the altar? What do I imply then? That food offered to idols is anything, or that an idol is anything? No, I imply that what pagans sacrifice they offer to demons and not to God. I do not want you to be partners with demons. You cannot drink the cup of the Lord and the cup of demons. You cannot partake of the table of the Lord and the table of demons. Shall we provoke the Lord to jealousy? Are we stronger than he? . . .

But in the following instructions I do not commend you, because when you come together it is not for the better but for the worse. For, in the first place, when you assemble as a church, I hear that there are divisions among you; and I partly believe it, for there must be factions among you in order that those who are genuine among you may be recognized. When you meet together, it is not the Lord's supper that you eat. For in eating, each one goes ahead with his own meal, and one is hungry and another is drunk. What! Do you not have houses to eat and drink in? Or do you despise the church of God and humiliate those who have nothing? What shall I say to you? Shall I commend you in this? No, I will not.

For I received from the Lord what I also delivered to you, that the Lord Jesus on the night when he was betrayed took bread, and when he had given thanks, he broke it, and said, "This is my body which is for you. Do this in remembrance of me." In the same way also the cup, after supper, saying, "This cup is the new covenant in my blood. Do this, as often as you drink it, in remembrance of me." For as often as you eat this bread and drink the cup, you proclaim the Lord's death until he comes.

Whoever, therefore, eats the bread or drinks the cup of the Lord in an unworthy manner will be guilty of profaning the body and blood of the Lord. Let a man examine himself, and so eat of the bread and drink of the cup. For any one who eats and drinks without discerning the body eats and drinks judgment upon himself. That is why many of you are weak and ill, and some have died. But if we judged ourselves truly, we should not be judged. But when we are judged by the Lord, we are chastened so that we may not be condemned along with the world.

So then, my brethren, when you come together to eat, wait for one another — if any one is hungry, let him eat at home — lest you come together to be condemned.

— 1 Cor 10:1-22; 11:17-34

Acts: The Breaking of the Bread

Here we find Luke's description of the Church in the wake of the first Christian Pentecost.

So those who received his word were baptized, and there were added that day about three thousand souls. And they devoted themselves to the apostles' teaching and fellowship, to the breaking of bread and the prayers.

And fear came upon every soul; and many wonders and signs were done through the apostles. And all who believed were together and had all things in common; and they sold their possessions and goods and distributed them to all, as any had need. And day by day, attending the temple together and breaking bread in their homes, they partook of food with glad and generous hearts, praising God and having favor with all the people. And the Lord added to their number day by day those who were being saved.

— ACTS 2:41-47

Hebrews: The Heavenly Jerusalem

The Letter to the Hebrews describes Christian worship as an awesome communion of heaven and earth. The imagery of angels and heavenly worship appears often in the Church's early liturgies.

For you have not come to what may be touched, a blazing fire, and darkness, and gloom, and a tempest, and the sound of a trumpet, and a voice whose words made the hearers entreat that no further messages be spoken to them. For they could not endure the order that was given, "If even a beast touches the mountain, it shall be stoned." Indeed, so terrifying was the sight that Moses said, "I tremble with fear." But you have come to Mount Zion and to the city of the living God, the heavenly Jerusalem, and to innumerable angels in festal gathering, and to the assembly of the first-born who are enrolled in heaven, and to a judge who is God of all, and to the spirits of just men made perfect, and to Jesus, the mediator of a new covenant, and to the sprinkled blood that speaks more graciously than the blood of Abel.

See that you do not refuse him who is speaking. For if they did not escape when they refused him who warned them on earth, much less shall we escape if we reject him who warns from heaven. His voice then shook the earth; but now he has promised, "Yet once more I will shake not only the earth but also the heaven." This phrase, "Yet once more," indicates the removal of what is shaken, as of what has been made, in order that what cannot be shaken may remain. Therefore let us be grateful for receiving a kingdom that cannot be shaken, and thus let us offer to God acceptable worship, with reverence and awe; for our God is a consuming fire.

— HEB 12:18-29

Revelation: The Liturgy of Heaven

John's Apocalypse describes heavenly worship in terms of the earthly worship most familiar to Christians: the hidden manna, the chalices, the vestments, and the incense of the Mass. John's description of heaven's court, for example, mirrored the arrangement of the bishop and his priests around the Church's altar in the early liturgy. John's hymns and chants reappear in many ancient liturgies. Almost all the early liturgical commentaries cite the Book of Revelation.

> After this I looked, and lo, in heaven an open door! And the first voice, which I had heard speaking to me like a trumpet, said, "Come up hither, and I will show you what must take place after this." At once I was in the Spirit, and lo, a throne stood in heaven, with one seated on the throne! And he who sat there appeared like jasper and carnelian, and round the throne was a rainbow that looked like an emerald. Round the throne were twenty-four thrones, and seated on the thrones were twenty-four elders [*presbuteroi*, "priests"], clad in white garments, with golden crowns upon their heads. From the throne issue flashes of lightning, and voices and peals of thunder, and before the throne burn seven torches of fire, which are the seven spirits of God; and before the throne there is as it were a sea of glass, like crystal.
>
> And round the throne, on each side of the throne, are four living creatures, full of eyes in front and behind: the first living creature like a lion, the second living creature like an ox, the third living creature with the face of a man, and the fourth living creature like a flying eagle. And the four living creatures, each of them with six wings, are full of eyes all round and within, and day and night they never cease to sing, "Holy, holy, holy is the Lord God Almighty, who was and is and is to come!" And whenever the living creatures give glory and honor and thanks to him who is seated on the throne, who lives for ever and ever, the twenty-four elders fall down before him who is seated on the throne and worship him who lives for ever and ever; they cast their crowns before the

throne, singing, "Worthy art thou, our Lord and God, to receive glory and honor and power, for thou didst create all things, and by thy will they existed and were created."

— REV 4:6-11

Revelation: The Marriage Supper of the Lamb

And the twenty-four elders [*presbuteroi*] and the four living creatures fell down and worshiped God who is seated on the throne, saying, "Amen. Hallelujah!" And from the throne came a voice crying, "Praise our God, all you his servants, you who fear him, small and great." Then I heard what seemed to be the voice of a great multitude, like the sound of many waters and like the sound of mighty thunderpeals, crying, "Hallelujah! For the Lord our God the Almighty reigns. Let us rejoice and exult and give him the glory, for the marriage of the Lamb has come, and his Bride has made herself ready; it was granted her to be clothed with fine linen, bright and pure" — for the fine linen is the righteous deeds of the saints.

And the angel said to me, "Write this: Blessed are those who are invited to the marriage supper of the Lamb." And he said to me, "These are true words of God."

—REV 19:4-9

CHAPTER 7

The *Didache*

The *Didache* (Greek for "Teaching") is probably the oldest Christian text, apart from Scripture, to survive till our day. Its full title in translation is *The Teaching of the Lord Through the Twelve Apostles to the Gentiles*.

The *Didache* represents the earliest of the genre of "Church orders" — wide-ranging documents that offer guidance in matters moral, legal, ascetical, and liturgical. Several of the later Church orders, such as the *Apostolic Constitutions*, incorporate sections of the *Didache* almost verbatim.

Three chapters of the *Didache* — chapters 9, 10, and 14 — deal specifically with the liturgy, advising the faithful how to prepare and conduct themselves, and prescribing prayers for the clergy. Enrico Mazza of the University of Milan argues persuasively that these chapters were composed no later than A.D. 48. He writes:

> The express conception of the Eucharist in *Didache* 9.2 supposes a Judeo-Christian Church with a primitive Christology, one that considers itself to be part ▪ of Judaism and its messianic expectations. This situation is no longer present at the time of the Council of Jerusalem [48-9 A.D.; see Acts 15] . . . Therefore I suggest that the two Eucharists of the *Didache* were composed before this date . . . 1 Corinthians is famil-

iar with and uses the eucharistic liturgy of the *Didache* and . . . bases itself on these texts of the *Didache* in order to express the eucharistic theology that Paul shares with the community at Corinth . . . Paul evangelized Corinth between 50 and 52.

— Mazza 1995: 40-41

If Mazza is correct, then the rites of the *Didache* may be older than all the books of the New Testament.

Chapters 9, 10, and 14, considered together, make clear that, even at this early date, the Church reserved Holy Communion only for those who were baptized and free of any grave sin: "Let no one eat or drink of your Eucharist unless they have been baptized. . . . If anyone is holy, let him come; if anyone is not so, let him repent." Repentance, we see in chapter 14, normally involves confession: "Give thanks after having confessed your transgressions, that your sacrifice may be pure."

Chapter 15 speaks of two orders of clergy — bishops and deacons — though it does not mention them in the context of the liturgy. From other early accounts, we know that the bishop ordinarily presided over the Sunday Eucharist of his particular Church; the deacons assisted in the distribution of the sacred elements and sometimes led the congregation in prayer. The document also acknowledges the presence of "prophets" in the congregation and allows them the freedom to "give thanks as much as they desire" (10). Both the role of prophets and the meaning of "give thanks" (*eucharistein*) in this context are obscure and have been given a variety of interpretations.

In the *Didache*'s prayers, Bouyer sees a clear extension of the spirituality of early Judaism; indeed, he argues that the anaphora and post-Communion may be composed of Jewish prayers lightly edited — adapted for Christian liturgy in light of the fullness of revelation in Jesus Christ (1968:115ff).

A minority of scholars hold that the *Didache* describes not a Eucharist but an *agape* meal, and that the word *eucharist*, used throughout, means a simple giving of thanks — a more elaborate grace for a most solemn meal (see, for example, Dix 1945:90ff). Still others discern an early rite that combined the Eucharist and *agape*, as in Corinth of Paul's time.

Cited often by early Christian writers, the *Didache* disappeared from view for many centuries and was known only through secondary citations. In 1875, a complete eleventh-century Greek manuscript surfaced in a library in Constantinople.

The *Didache* invokes the authority of the apostles and of Jesus himself. While such attribution may be merely a literary convention, the *Didache* could also represent an authentic record of Christian origins, compiled in Antioch, the city where the disciples "were for the first time called Christians" (Acts 11:26).

The excerpts below are based on the 1884 translation of Isaac H. Hall and John T. Napier.

A Eucharistic Prayer

Chapter 9 of the *Didache* seems to record a very early eucharistic prayer, with blessings over the cup and the bread. Conspicuously absent from the text is the traditional narrative of institution, the account of the Last Supper with Christ's words "This is my body. . . . This is the cup of my blood." It is possible that some early eucharistic prayers lacked these phrases. They are absent from the extant manuscripts of at least ten early eucharistic prayers (Taft 2003). It is also possible, though less likely, that the clergy customarily recited the institution narrative from memory.

Now concerning the Eucharist, give thanks this way.

First, concerning the cup: "We thank you, our Father, for the holy vine of David your servant, which you made known to us through Jesus your servant; to you be the glory for ever."

And concerning the broken bread: "We thank you, our Father, for the life and knowledge which you made known to us through Jesus your servant; to you be the glory for ever. Even as this broken bread was scattered over the hills, and was gathered together and became one, so let your Church be gathered together from the ends of the earth into your kingdom; for yours is the glory and the power through Jesus Christ for ever."

But let no one eat or drink of your Eucharist unless they have been baptized into the name of the Lord; for concerning this also the Lord has said, "Give not that which is holy to the dogs."

— CHAPTER 9

Thanksgiving

Most readers see in chapter 10 of the *Didache* (below) a post-Communion prayer, since the rubric indicates that it should be recited "after you are filled."

But after you are filled, give thanks this way:

"We thank you, holy Father, for your holy name which you caused to dwell in our hearts, and for the knowledge and faith and immortality, which you made known to us through Jesus your servant; to you be the glory for ever.

"Almighty Master, you created all things for your name's sake; you gave food and drink to men for enjoyment, that they might give thanks to you; but to us you freely gave spiritual food and drink and life eternal through your servant. Before all things we thank you that you are mighty; to you be the glory for ever.

"Remember, Lord, your Church, to deliver it from all evil and to make it perfect in your love, and gather it from the four winds, sanctified for your kingdom which you have prepared for it; for yours is the power and the glory for ever.

"Let grace come, and let this world pass away. Hosanna to the God (Son) of David! If any one is holy, let him come; if any one is not so, let him repent. Maranatha. Amen."

But permit the prophets to give thanks as much as they desire.

— CHAPTER 10

The Confession of Sins

Chapter 14 records a valuable early witness to the sacrificial nature of the Eucharist. The word sacrifice appears three times in a short space, and the author quotes the prophet Malachi, whose passages on Temple sacrifice were seen by the early Christian Fathers as foreshadowing the Eucharist, the always-and-everywhere sacrifice of Christ (see, for example, the passages from Justin and Irenaeus included in this book).

Every Lord's day gather yourselves together and break bread, and give thanks after having confessed your transgressions, that your sacrifice may be pure. But let no one who is at odds with his fellow come together with you, until they be reconciled, that your sacrifice may not be profaned. For this is that which was spoken by the Lord:

"In every place and time offer to me a pure sacrifice; for I am a great king, says the Lord, and my name is feared among the nations" (see Mal 1:11, 14).

— CHAPTER 14

CHAPTER 8

St. Clement of Rome

Pope Clement of Rome is a shadowy figure about whom we know very little; and historians hotly dispute even the little we think we might know. His *Letter to the Corinthians*, however, surely belongs among the handful of artifacts that are most important for early Church history. For it is certainly one of the most ancient Christian documents to survive into our times.

Historians commonly refer to the letter as *1 Clement*. Another text is attributed to Clement, but it probably originated with a different Roman author at a slightly later date. All responsible estimates place *1 Clement* in the first century, but within a relatively wide range: between A.D. 67 and 96. Msgr. Thomas Herron follows John A.T. Robinson in placing it early, before A.D. 70 (Herron 1988; Robinson 1976). Herron finds eleven instances where Clement's letter sheds light on the dating question. Most persuasive is that Clement seems to assume that the Jerusalem Temple is still standing and still offering daily sacrifices. Roman troops destroyed the city and the sanctuary in A.D. 70.

The difficulty in dating *1 Clement* comes partly because of discrepancies in the ancient records. Clement appears as the fourth pope — after Peter, Linus, and Anencletus — on several early lists, including those of Hegesippus and Irenaeus in the second century, and Eusebius in the early fourth century.

The anonymous Roman *Liberian Catalogue*, however, places him third on the list.

It is a difference of less than thirty years, but those were crucial decades for the development of Christian doctrine and discipline, and *1 Clement* touches on many important matters of doctrine and discipline. So the dating of this letter can have a great influence on our reading of early Church history.

1 Clement is a long letter, well attested in antiquity. Polycarp and Irenaeus quote it in the second century. Clement of Alexandria uses it extensively in the third. Some ancient authors treat it as inspired Scripture, and many of the early copies we possess are bound in with other books of the New Testament. There is ample evidence that the letter was revered universally. Copies survive in Greek, Latin, Syriac, and Coptic.

The early tradition is unanimous in ascribing the letter to Pope Clement I, though his name appears nowhere in the text. Officially, the letter is from "the Church of God which sojourns at Rome" to "the Church of God which sojourns at Corinth." It was occasioned by the Corinthian congregation's appeal to the Roman Church for intervention in a local dispute. The Corinthians were contending among themselves over the offices of the clergy.

Clement responded with a long and irenic letter, exhorting the faraway Christians to "harmony." He shows that God has established an order in creation, ordaining the inexorable succession of seasons. He demonstrates also, from the Old Testament, that God intended his people to observe a certain order in life and worship. He goes on, then, to show that Christ provided clear guidelines for order in the Church's hierarchy and liturgy. The priestly offices, the altar, and the Eucharist have been established by God, not by any human devising. Thus, contention in these matters is more than unseemly; it is sinful.

Dionysius, the bishop of Corinth around A.D.170 , records that his congregations were still reading Clement's letter in the liturgy.

The excerpts below are based on the translation in the 1892 Edinburgh edition of the Fathers and J.B. Lightfoot's Greek and English versions in *The Apostolic Fathers.*

Everything in Its Proper Place

All these things are clear to us who have looked into the depths of the divine knowledge. We should do all things in their proper order, which the Lord has commanded us to perform at the stated times. He has commanded offerings to be presented and services to be performed, not in a thoughtless or irregular way, but at the appointed times and hours. Moreover, he himself has fixed by his own supreme will where and by whom he wants these things to be done, so that all things should be piously done according to his good pleasure and may be acceptable to him. Therefore, those who present their offerings at the appointed times are accepted and blessed; for inasmuch as they follow the laws of the Lord, they do not sin. For the high priest has his own particular services assigned to him, and priests have theirs assigned to them, as the Levites, too, have their own special ministries. The layman is bound by the laws that pertain to laymen.

Let every one of you, my brothers, offer Eucharist to God according to his own order — with a clear conscience and proper reverence, and not going beyond the rules of the ministry prescribed to him. Not in every place, my brothers, are the daily sacrifices offered, or the peace-offerings, or the sin-offerings and the trespass-offerings, but in Jerusalem only. And even there they are not offered in any place, but only at the altar before the temple. That which is offered is first carefully examined by the high priest and the ministers already mentioned. Those, therefore, who do anything beyond what conforms to his will are punished with death. You see, my brothers, that the greater the knowledge that has been given to us, the greater also is the danger to which we are exposed.

The apostles preached the Gospel to us from the Lord Jesus Christ; and Jesus Christ was sent by God. Thus, Christ was commissioned by God, and the apostles by Christ. Both these appointments were made in an orderly way, according to the will of God. Once the apostles had received their orders and were fully assured by the resurrection of our Lord Jesus Christ, they went forth — established in the word of God, with full assurance of the Holy Spirit — proclaiming that the kingdom of God was at hand. Preaching through countries and cities, they appointed the first-fruits of their labors — after first proving them by the Spirit — to be bishops and deacons of those who should afterwards believe. Nor was this anything new, since many ages before it was written concerning bishops and deacons. For so says the Scripture in a certain place, "I will appoint their bishops in righteousness, and their deacons in faith" (Is 60:17 in the Greek *Septuagint*).

It should not surprise us that those Christians whom God entrusted with this duty should make such appointments. For blessed Moses, who "was faithful in all God's house as a servant" (Heb 3:5), noted in the sacred books all the instructions that were given to him. And the other prophets that followed him also bear consistent witness to the instructions he established. When rivalry arose over the priesthood (see Num 16-18), and the tribes contended over which should be adorned with that glorious title, he commanded the twelve princes of the tribes to bring him their staffs, each one inscribed with the name of the tribe. He took them, bound them together, and sealed them with the rings of the princes of the tribes. Then, placing them in the tabernacle of witness on the table of God, he shut the doors of the tabernacle and sealed the keys, as he had sealed the rods. Then he said to them, "Men and brothers, the tribe whose rod shall blossom is the one God has chosen to fulfill the office of the priesthood and to serve him." In the morning, he assembled all Israel, six hundred thousand men. He showed the seals to the princes of the tribes, and he opened the tabernacle of witness and brought forth the staffs. And Aaron's staff had not only blossomed, but borne fruit. What do you think of that, my beloved? Did not Moses know beforehand that this would happen? Surely he knew; but he acted this way, so that there might be no disorder in Israel, and so that the name of the true and only God might be glorified. To him be glory for ever and ever. Amen.

Our apostles also knew, through our Lord Jesus Christ, that there would be strife over the office of bishop. In their perfect foreknowledge, they appointed those ministers already mentioned. Afterwards they gave instructions that, when these men should fall asleep, other approved men should succeed them in their ministry. We hold, therefore, that those who were appointed by them, or afterwards by other eminent men, with the consent of the whole Church — those who have blamelessly served the flock of Christ in a humble, peaceful, and disinterested spirit, and who have long enjoyed the approval of everyone — cannot be justly dismissed from the ministry. For our sin will not be small if we remove from the office of bishop those who have fulfilled its duties in a blameless and holy way.

— CHAPTERS 40-44

CHAPTER 9

St. Ignatius of Antioch

The biography of Ignatius (d. 107) can be summed up by two facts: He was bishop of Antioch in Syria, and he was condemned to die in Rome. We know nothing of his acts while he held office — though we can assume that, as bishop, he was the principal celebrant of the liturgy in a metropolis that was the "second city of the empire" and a vibrant center of the newborn faith.

There is much more we can infer, however, from the seven letters he wrote on the journey across Asia Minor to his martyrdom. He was a passionate man. He held his authority confidently. He nurtured a deep love for Jesus Christ and the Church; and he was unabashed in expressing his burning hatred for heresy.

The Eucharist is the beating heart of Ignatius' teaching. Though he seems to observe strict silence regarding liturgical texts, he did, in several places, expound a lively pastoral theology of the Eucharist.

He echoed the sacrificial language of the *Didache*, speaking of the Church as the "place of sacrifice," the "sanctuary of the altar." The bishop presided over the sacrifice, and it is at this altar that the Church received its unity in Christ. "For there is one flesh of our Lord Jesus Christ, and one cup to show forth the unity of his blood; one altar, as there is one bishop" (*Philadelphians* 4). As far as we know, Ignatius was the first to call the Church "Catholic" (*Smyrnaeans* 8).

Ignatius identified the denial of the Eucharist as the very mark of heresy. Heretics are those who "abstain from the Eucharist and from prayer, because they do not confess the Eucharist to be the flesh of our Savior Jesus Christ" (*Smyrnaeans* 7). Heretical ideas, moreover, had consequences in the social order; for the heretics "have no regard for love; no care for the widow, the orphan, or the oppressed; the enslaved or the free; the hungry or the thirsty" (ibid.).

The direst wage of heresy, though, is death. Ignatius followed Paul (see 1 Cor 11:30) in warning that those who disdain Communion bring about their own dissolution, both spiritual and physical: "Those, therefore, who speak against this gift of God, incur death" (*Smyrnaeans* 7). Only full repentance could restore them to the sacrament, which elsewhere he called "the medicine of immortality and the antidote to prevent us from dying" (*Ephesians* 20).

Ignatius counseled Christians to shun heretics, who should not be admitted to the Communion that they denied both in its essence and in its effects. Moreover, according to Ignatius, the Church would not recognize as valid the worship of the heretics: "Let that be deemed a proper Eucharist which is administered either by the bishop or by one to whom he has entrusted it" (*Smyrnaeans* 8).

Like the *Didache*, Ignatius' letters point to the bishop as the ordinary minister of the Eucharist. Also in Ignatius, we first encounter the order of "priest," or presbyter, mentioned among the orders of the clergy.

An early tradition holds that Ignatius was a disciple of the apostle John, and the eucharistic spirituality of the letters would seem to give this credence. For Ignatius, as for John, the "bread of life" was the only sure antidote to everlasting death: "Unless you eat the flesh of the Son of man and drink his blood, you have no life in you. . . . He who eats this bread will live forever" (Jn 6:53, 58).

As he approached the execution of his sentence, Ignatius identified himself more and more with the sacrifice of the altar. He left the Church of Rome perhaps the most beautiful and moving metaphor for the self-sacrifice of martyrdom: "I am the wheat of God. Let me be ground by the teeth of the wild beasts, that I may be found the pure bread of Christ" (*Romans* 4).

The following excerpts are based on the translation of Ignatius' letters in the 1892 Edinburgh edition of the Fathers of the Church.

Communion and Excommunication

Let no man deceive himself. For both the beings of heaven, the glorious angels, and the rulers, both seen and unseen, incur condemnation if they do not believe in the blood of Christ. . . . Consider those who hold a different opinion regarding the grace of Christ that has come to us — how opposed they are to the will of God. They have no regard for love; no care for the widow, the orphan, or the oppressed; the enslaved or the free; the hungry or the thirsty.

They abstain from the Eucharist and from prayer, because they do not confess the Eucharist to be the flesh of our Savior Jesus Christ, which suffered for our sins, and which the Father, in His goodness, raised up again. Those, therefore, who speak against this gift of God, incur death in the midst of their disputes. Yet it would be better for them to treat it with respect, that they also might rise again.

It is fitting, therefore, that you should keep aloof from such persons, and not to speak of them either in private or in public, but to give heed to the prophets, and above all to the Gospel, in which the passion has been revealed to us, and the resurrection has been fully proved. But avoid all divisions, as the beginning of evils. . . .

See that you follow the bishop, even as Jesus Christ follows the Father. Follow the priests as you would follow the apostles. And reverence the deacons as you would reverence the command of God. Let no man do anything connected with the Church without the bishop. Let that be deemed a proper Eucharist which is administered either by the bishop or by one to whom he has entrusted it. Wherever the bishop shall appear, there let the assembly also be — just as, wherever Jesus Christ is, there is the Catholic Church. Apart from the bishop, it is not lawful to baptize or to celebrate an *agape*. But whatever he shall approve is pleasing to God, so that everything that is done may be secure and valid.

— *SMYRNAEANS* 6-8

Praise of Unity

If I, in this brief space of time, have enjoyed such fellowship with your bishop — I mean not of a mere human, but of a spiritual nature — how much more do I consider you happy who are so joined to him as the Church is to Jesus Christ, and as Jesus Christ is to the Father, that so all things may agree in unity! Let no man deceive himself: if any one be not within the altar, he is deprived of the bread of God. For if the prayer of one or two possesses such power, how much more that of the bishop and the whole Church! He, therefore, who does not assemble with the Church, has thus manifested his pride and condemned himself. For it is written, "God resists the proud" (1 Pt 5:5). Let us be careful, then, not to set ourselves in opposition to the bishop, in order that we may be subject to God.

— *Ephesians* 5

The Poison of Heresy

I beg you — yet not I, but the love of Jesus Christ — to use only Christian nourishment, and abstain from food of a different kind: that is, heresy. For those who mix up Jesus Christ with their own poison and speak discreditable things are like those who administer a deadly drug in sweet wine. The ignorant man takes it in greedily, with a fatal pleasure leading to his own death.

Be on guard, then, against such persons. And this will be the case with you if you are not puffed up, and if you remain in intimate union with Jesus Christ our God, and the bishop, and the enactments of the apostles. He who is near the altar is pure, but he who is apart is impure. He who does anything apart from the bishop, the priests, and deacons, is not pure in his conscience.

Not that I know there is anything of this kind among you; but I put you on your guard, because I love you dearly, and I foresee the snares of the devil. So, clothing yourselves with meekness, be renewed in faith, that is the flesh of the Lord, and in love, that is the blood of Jesus Christ. Let none of you cherish any grudge against his neighbor. Give no occasion to the gentiles, lest by means of a few foolish men the whole multitude in God be derided.

— *Trallians* 6-8

'With the Bishop'

Keep yourselves from those evil plants that Jesus Christ does not tend, because they are not the planting of the Father. Not that I have found any division among you, but exceeding purity. For all those who belong to God and to Jesus Christ are also with the bishop. And all those who repent and return to the unity of the Church shall also belong to God, that they may live according to Jesus Christ. Do not be deceived, my brethren. If anyone follows a man who makes a schism in the Church, he shall not inherit the kingdom of God. If anyone walks according to a strange opinion, he disagrees with the passion [of Christ].

Take care, then, to have only one Eucharist. For there is one flesh of our Lord Jesus Christ, and one cup to show forth the unity of his blood; one altar, as there is one bishop, along with the priests and deacons, my fellow servants. All this is so, so that, whatever you do, you may do it according to the will of God.

PHILADELPHIANS 3-4

CHAPTER 10

———

Pliny the Younger

What was the crime of Christians during the age of Roman persecution? According to the pagan governor of Pontus-Bithynia (in what is now Turkey), "the whole of their guilt" was summed up in their attendance of the Sunday liturgy. For the Christians, by their very act of worship, "bound themselves by a solemn oath" to a way of life that permitted worship of only one God. This commitment kept them from fulfilling their civic duty, mandated by law, to worship the Roman emperor and his guiding spirit, his "genius."

Around the year 112, after conducting a careful forensic investigation — which included interrogations and torture — Pliny the Younger relayed his findings to Emperor Trajan in the bland terms of a bureaucrat's report. Yet this small document yields rare information about worship at the opening of the second century.

Christians met, he said, "on a certain fixed day before it was light, when they sang in alternate verses a hymn to Christ . . . and bound themselves by a solemn oath." Thus, we learn that the early Church worshiped with music sung in antiphons, by call and response.

Pliny's use of the word oath is curious and has been the subject of controversy in recent years. The Latin word is *sacramentum*, and Pliny's reporting could reflect the Church's very early application of the term "sacrament" to describe the mysteries of faith.

According to Pliny, the Church's Sunday worship consisted of two meetings. The Christians would "disperse" and then "reassemble" at a later time to partake of "food" of an "ordinary kind." The passage is obscure. Some commentators find evidence here to suggest that, in the beginning, the Church kept the Liturgy of the Word as a rite distinct and discrete from the Liturgy of the Eucharist. Others contend, rather, that Pliny was describing the full eucharistic liturgy followed by the agape later in the day.

The governor's observation that the Church's ritual food was "of an ordinary and innocent kind" suggests that some pagans had claimed otherwise. Indeed, in other sources we find that Christians often faced outrageous charges about the worship they conducted in secrecy — charges of cannibalism, infanticide, and sexual license. Pliny concluded, however, that the crime of the Christians was much more mundane — he calls it "political" — though nonetheless punishable by death. The crime of the sacramentum was sedition.

The following is adapted from Pliny Letters (1915), translated by William Melmoth and revised by W.M.L. Hutchinson.

A Report from the Provincial Governor

It is a rule, sir, which I inviolably observe, to refer myself to you in all my doubts; for who is more capable of guiding my uncertainty or informing my ignorance? I have never attended any trials of Christians, and so I am unacquainted with the method and limits to be observed in examining or punishing them. Thus, I am unsure as to whether any difference is to be made on account of age, or no distinction allowed between the youngest and the adult; whether repentance admits to a pardon, or if a man has been once a Christian it does him no good to recant; whether the mere profession of Christianity, even without crimes, or only the crimes associated with Christianity are punishable.

Meanwhile, this is the method I have observed toward those who have been denounced to me as Christians: I interrogated them as to whether they were Christians; if they confessed it, I repeated the question twice again, adding the threat of capital punishment; if they still persevered, I ordered them to be executed. For whatever the nature of their creed might be, I could at least feel no doubt that such contempt and inflexible obstinacy deserved punishment. There were others also possessed with the same infatuation, but since they were Roman citizens, I directed them to be carried to Rome.

These accusations spread (as is usually the case) from the mere fact of the matter being investigated, and several forms of the mischief came to light. An anonymous placard was put up, accusing a large number of persons by name. I thought it proper to release those who denied they were, or had ever been, Christians, who repeated after me an invocation to the gods, and who offered adoration, with wine and incense, to your image, which I had ordered to be brought for that purpose together with images of the gods, and who finally cursed Christ. None of these acts, it is said, real Christians can be forced to perform. Others who were named by that informer at first confessed to be Christians, and then denied it; true, they had been of that persuasion, but they had abandoned it, some three years, others many years, and a few as long as twenty-five years ago. They all worshiped your statue and the images of the gods, and cursed Christ.

They affirmed, however, that the whole of their guilt, or error, was that they were in the habit of meeting on a certain fixed day before it was light, when they sang in alternate verses a hymn to Christ, as to a god, and bound themselves by a solemn oath, not to any wicked deeds, but never to commit any fraud, theft or adultery, never to falsify their word, nor deny a trust when they should be called upon to deliver it up. Afterward, it was their custom to disperse, and then reassemble to partake of food — but food of an ordinary and innocent kind. Even this practice, however, they had abandoned after the publication of my edict, by which, according to your orders, I had forbidden political associations. I judged it all the more necessary to extract the real truth, by means of torture, from two female slaves, who were styled deaconesses. But I could discover nothing more than depraved and excessive superstition.

I therefore adjourned the proceedings, and betook myself at once to your counsel. For the matter seemed to me well worth referring to you — especially considering the numbers endangered. Persons of all ranks and ages, and of both sexes, are, and will be, involved in the prosecution. For this contagious superstition is not confined to the cities only, but has spread through the villages and rural districts; it seems possible, however, to check and cure it.

It is certain at least that the temples, which had been almost deserted, are now beginning to be frequented; and the sacred festivals, after a long intermission, are again revived; and there is a general demand for sacrificial animals, which for some time past have met with but few purchasers. Hence, it is easy to imagine what multitudes may be reclaimed from this error, if a door be left open to repentance.

The Emperor's Reply

You have pursued, my dear Pliny, a very proper method in sifting the cases of those denounced to you as Christians. It is not possible to lay down any general rule that can be applied as the fixed standard in all cases of this nature. No search should be made for these people. When they are denounced and found guilty, they must be punished — with the restriction, however, that when the party denies he is a Christian, and gives proof that he is not (that is, by adoring our gods), he shall be pardoned on the ground of repentance, even though he may have formerly incurred suspicion. Anonymous accusations must not be admitted as evidence against anyone; for this introduces a very dangerous precedent, which does not conform to the spirit of the age.

CHAPTER 11

St. Justin Martyr

Our most complete description of the early Church's Mass, as it was celebrated in the West, comes from Justin, who set it down for Roman Emperor Antoninus Pius around the year 155.

Justin wrote from Rome, but he was a Samaritan by birth, pagan by upbringing, and a philosopher by vocation. His route to the Church and the city of Rome included many loops and detours.

An earnest seeker from a young age, Justin pursued wisdom in several of the major philosophical schools of his time — Stoic, Peripatetic, Pythagorean, Platonist. Yet all failed to satisfy him. One day, while walking on the beach, he encountered an old man who told him of the prophets of Israel. That conversation set Justin on a course from which he would never turn back, a course that culminated in his encounter with what he called the "philosophy" of Jesus Christ.

Justin was a philosopher, but not a rationalist. When he spoke of "philosophy," he intended the word in its root meaning: the love of wisdom. And the highest wisdom, for Justin, included the mysteries of faith, the sacraments, and the liturgy.

Justin spent the rest of his days as a wandering teacher, in the tradition of the major philosophical schools. He passed from town to town, explaining and defending Christian doctrine in public debate and in his writing. Through this work, he earned his place in history as the first great Christian apologist.

As he traveled, he encountered many misunderstandings about the Church's doctrine and worship. Some, perhaps, could have resulted from the traditional Christian reticence about the mysteries. Believers did, after all, conduct rituals that were closed to outsiders, and their Scriptures spoke of eating Jesus' flesh and drinking his blood. Such behavior must have seemed odd, even in lands where mystery cults abounded. Further distorted by the gossip of bigots, the rumors about Christianity must have grown frightful indeed.

Journeying to the imperial city, Justin discovered that such misunderstandings reached even to the heights of earthly power: the emperor and the Roman senate. Justin took it upon himself to write a rational defense — in Latin, *apologia* — of Christian faith and life. In English, this body of writings is usually called Justin's *Apologies* (divided into the *First* and *Second Apology*). In choosing which topics he would cover, Justin likely focused on the matters that were most essential and those that were most controversial. Certainly the Mass fell into both categories, for its explication takes up almost three full chapters in the *Apologies*.

In fact, Justin provided detailed descriptions of two Roman liturgies: first, a Mass that included a baptism; and second, a regular Sunday Mass. There are slight differences between the two. Both are reproduced here.

Justin described a Mass that looks familiar to modern Catholics in the West — partly because religious ritual is by nature conservative, and the parts of the Mass have remained essentially the same through the centuries, but also because Justin's account greatly influenced the reform of the Roman rite in the twentieth century.

In Justin's *Apologies*, we read of the sign of peace, the Gospel reading, the prayers of the faithful, the offertory, the great Amen, the Communion, and the collection. Compared to his predecessors, Justin is surprisingly frank, even addressing the doctrine of the Real Presence. He does, however, refrain from quoting liturgical texts at any length; this is, perhaps, his way of respecting the discipline of the secret. The two exceptions are the Amen, which he translates from Hebrew, and, very surprisingly, the words of institution, which other ancient writers scrupulously avoid: "This is my body. . . . This is my blood." It is possible that Justin, as an apologist, believed that such openness would help overcome ignorance and quell the rumors of ritual cannibalism. Justin makes clear, after all, that, though the priest says, "This is my body," what he distributes are the "eucharisted" elements of bread and wine.

Consistent with the *Didache,* the Book of Revelation, and the report of Pliny, Justin informs his readers that Sunday is the normal day of Christian worship.

It is in another work, however, that Justin shows an even more striking consistency with his predecessors. In his *Dialogue with Trypho*, Justin uses a Platonic literary form, a dramatized conversation, to demonstrate that the religion of Israel was brought to fulfillment in Christianity. His foil in the dialogue is a rabbi named Trypho, who argues the positions of the Jews then dispersed throughout the empire.

The Mass occupies a crucial place in the *Dialogue,* for Justin holds that the sacrifices of ancient Israel were Old Testament "types" that foreshadowed a New Testament fulfillment in the sacrifice of the Mass. "The offering of fine flour . . . prescribed as an offering on behalf of those purified from leprosy (Lev 14:10) was a type of the bread of the Eucharist" (*Dialogue* 41).

Again like the *Didache* and Ignatius, Justin goes on to quote the prophet Malachi, who had foretold an age when perfect sacrifice would be offered continually everywhere on earth. Trypho, in turn, argues that the recent dispersion of the Jews, in the year 70, was a providential preparation for the spiritual sacrifice to be offered always and everywhere. The Jews in exile raised the sacrifice by their lives of prayer.

Yet, for Justin, this answer does not suffice. God had, after all, rejected the material sacrifices of the Israelites in the time of Malachi. Why would God now accept the spiritual sacrifices of the Jews who were banished from Jerusalem? For Justin, only the Mass is a "perfect and acceptable sacrifice," because it is the sacrifice of the Incarnate Word himself, and not of sinful men. Moreover, Justin responds that the Jews' dispersion has not adequately fulfilled Malachi's prophecy of a universal sacrifice.

Justin's own sacrifice was completed when he died for the faith, beheaded by Roman authorities, around 165.

The following passages are adapted from the 1892 Edinburgh edition of the Fathers.

Mass After a Baptism

After we have washed someone who has been convinced and has accepted our teaching, we bring him to the place where those who are called "brethren" are assembled. Together, then, we offer hearty prayers for ourselves, for the enlightened [baptized] person, and for all others in every place. . . . After the prayers, we greet one another with a kiss. Then bread and a cup of wine mixed with water are brought to the president of the brethren. Taking them, he gives praise and glory to the Father of the universe, through the name of the Son and of the Holy Spirit, and he offers thanks at considerable length that we have been counted worthy to receive these things from his hands.

When he has concluded the prayers and thanksgivings, all the people present express their assent by saying "Amen." This word is Hebrew for "so be it." And when the president has given thanks, and all the people have expressed their assent, those whom we call deacons distribute to each of those present a portion of the bread and the wine mixed with water, over which the thanksgiving was pronounced. To those who are absent, they carry away a portion.

This food we call the Eucharist, and no one is allowed to partake but the man who believes that our doctrines are true, who has been washed with the bath for the remission of sins and rebirth, and who is living as Christ has commanded.

We do not receive these as common bread and drink. For Jesus Christ our Savior, made flesh by the Word of God, had both flesh and blood for our salvation. Likewise, we have been taught that the food blessed by the prayer of his word — and from which our own blood and flesh are nourished and changed — is the flesh and blood of Jesus who was made flesh.

The apostles, in the memoirs they composed called "Gospels," have passed on to us what was given to them: that Jesus took bread, and when he had given thanks, said, "Do this in memory of me. This is my body." In the same way, after taking the cup and giving thanks, he said, "This is my blood," and he gave it to them alone.

This the wicked devils have imitated, commanding the same thing to be done in the mysteries of Mithras. There, in the mystic rites of initiation, bread and a cup of water are placed amid certain incantations. This you already know or can find out.

— *FIRST APOLOGY* 65-66

Sunday Mass in Rome

On the day called Sunday, all who live in cities or country-side gather in one place, and the memoirs of the apostles or the writings of the prophets are read, as long as time permits. Then, when the reader has finished, the president instructs and exhorts them to imitate these good things. Then we all rise together and pray. . . . When our prayer is ended, bread and wine with water are brought forth, and the president offers prayers and thanksgivings, according to his ability. The people assent, saying "Amen"; and there is a distribution to each of the eucharistic elements. The deacons carry a portion to those who are absent.

Those who are able give willingly whatever sum they each think appropriate. The money collected is deposited with the president. He gives it, then, to comfort orphans, widows, and those who are wanting, through sickness or any other cause, and those who are imprisoned, and strangers traveling among us. In a word, he takes care of all who are in need.

Sunday is when we hold our assembly because it is the first day, on which God brought forth the world from darkness and matter. On the same day, Jesus Christ our Savior rose from the dead. For he was crucified on the day before Saturn's day (Saturday); and on the day after Saturn's day, which is the day of the sun, he appeared to his apostles and disciples and taught them these things, which we have submitted to you for your consideration.

— *FIRST APOLOGY* 67

A Glimpse in the Old Testament

The offering of fine flour, . . . which was prescribed as an offering on behalf of those purified from leprosy (Lev 14:10), was a type of the bread of the Eucharist. Our Lord Jesus Christ prescribed this celebration in memory of the suffering he endured for those whose souls are purified from evil. At this time, we also thank God for creating the world and all things in it, and for man, and for delivering us from our former evil, and utterly overthrowing angelic principalities and powers by him who suffered according to his will.

So, as I said before, God speaks by the mouth of Malachi, one of the twelve [prophets], about the sacrifices you offered at that time: "I have no pleasure in you, says the Lord of hosts, and I will not accept an offering from your hand. For from the rising of the sun to its setting my name is great among the nations, and in every place incense is offered to my name, and a pure offering; for my name is great among the nations, says the Lord of hosts, but you profane it" (Mal 1:10-12).

He speaks here of those Gentiles, namely us, who everywhere offer him sacrifices — that is, the bread of the Eucharist and the cup of the Eucharist, affirming both that we glorify his name and that you profane it. . . .

— *DIALOGUE* 41

The Perfect and Acceptable Sacrifice

We are the true high-priestly family of God. God himself bears witness to this, when he says that, everywhere among the Gentiles, sacrifices are offered to him well-pleasing and pure. Now God receives sacrifices from no one except through his priests.

Anticipating all the sacrifices we offer through this name — the sacrifices Jesus Christ enjoined us to offer in the Eucharist of the bread and cup — the sacrifices now offered by Christians everywhere throughout the world — God bears witness that they are well-pleasing to him. But he utterly rejects those presented by you and by those priests of yours, saying, "I will not accept an offering from your hand. For from the rising of the sun to its setting my name is great among the nations, and in every place incense is offered to my name, and a pure offering; for my name is great among the nations, says the Lord of hosts, but you profane it" (Mal 1:10-12).

Yet, even now, you love contention. You assert that God did not accept the sacrifices of those who lived in Jerusalem and were called Israelites, but he is pleased now with the prayers of those dispersed from that nation — and he calls their prayers sacrifices!

Now, I, too, admit that prayers and thanksgiving, when offered by worthy men, are the only perfect and acceptable sacrifice to God. And these alone are what Christians offer in the memorial made by their food and drink. These elements call to mind the suffering of the Son of God, whose name the high priests of your nation and your teachers have caused to be profaned and blasphemed over all the earth. But God shows that these filthy garments — which you have placed on those who have become Christians by the name of Jesus — these shall be taken away from us when he shall raise all men from the dead and appoint some to be incorruptible, immortal, and free from sorrow in the everlasting and imperishable kingdom. But others he shall send away to the everlasting punishment of fire.

You and your teachers deceive yourselves when you interpret what the Scripture says as referring to those dispersed members of your nation — when you maintain that their prayers and sacrifices offered in every place are pure and well-pleasing. Learn that you are speaking falsely and cheating yourselves. For, first of all, not even now does your nation extend from the rising to the setting of the sun; there are nations among which none of your race ever lived.

Yet there is not one single race of men — whether barbarians, Greeks, or whatever; nomads, vagrants, or herdsmen living in tents — among whom prayers and thanksgiving are not offered through the name of the crucified Jesus.

— DIALOGUE 117

CHAPTER 12

St. Irenaeus of Lyons

Irenaeus is a pivotal figure in the history of the early Church. Born in Smyrna (Izmir in modern Turkey), he passed his childhood as an attentive disciple of the elderly bishop Polycarp (d. 156), who in his own youth had received the Gospel from John the Apostle. Thus, Irenaeus's work serves as a bridge between the apostolic age and the time of the later Fathers. Moreover, as an Easterner who spent his most productive years in the West, he also spans two Christian cultures that, even in the second century, were already quite distinct.

From Smyrna, Irenaeus somehow made his way westward to Lyons in Gaul (modern France), where he served as bishop until the end of the second century. His writings show that he had a keen awareness of his privileged training — his nearness to the apostle John. Yet with Irenaeus's privilege came the duty of preserving and protecting what he had received. And so he wrote voluminously in defense of true doctrine and against the various heresies and schisms that were cropping up in the Church.

His greatest work is the massive *Against Heresies*, a refutation of the polymorphous doctrines of Gnosticism, the most prevalent heresy of his day. Gnostic sects preached a dizzying variety of myths and rituals, drawing selectively from the elements of Christian doctrine. Most of these sects emphasized a pseudo-mystical "knowledge" (in Greek, *gnosis*) intended only for the spiritual elite. Most also believed that the material world was evil. Indeed, according to Gnostic myths, the world was created by a wicked demigod — some said it was Yahweh, the God of Israel — in order to imprison the spirits of light, with whom the Gnostics identified themselves.

For the Gnostic, there could be no redemption of matter, because matter was radically evil and radically opposed to the spirit of the true god. Hatred of creation led most of these sects to reject the doctrine of the Incarnation of the Word as well as the sacraments of the Church, all of which employed material elements — bread, wine, water, oil — for spiritual ends. What, after all, could matter have to do with spirit? Most Gnostics also rejected the resurrection of the body, for Christ and for all believers. In Gnostic theology, the flesh was a prison from which the divine light must escape forever. Resurrection, then, could only be further entrapment.

Irenaeus intended his *Against Heresies* to be a thoroughgoing analysis of all the major Gnostic systems. Yet it was more than an attack. In responding to the Gnostics, Irenaeus became perhaps the first churchman to compose a comprehensive, systematic theological reflection on Christian doctrine.

Central to Irenaeus's theology is the idea, drawn from Paul's Letter to the Romans, of "recapitulation." By taking on human flesh, Jesus Christ recovered what Adam had lost through original sin. Thus, Christ restored and rehabilitated the human race and renewed the whole world. Christians, then, represent a new creation.

In this context, Irenaeus discusses the meaning of the Eucharist. In the world before Christ, God had commanded man to offer a pure sacrifice of the "first-fruits" of the earth. Sinful man, however, proved unable to offer with a pure heart. So Christ established the Eucharist as "the new oblation of the new covenant." In the Eucharist, Christ himself is the offering (the "first-fruits" of the new creation), and Christ himself is the one who offers.

For Irenaeus, the sacrifice of the Church is the fulfillment of all the sacrifices of ancient Israel. Consistent with the *Didache* and with Justin, he invokes the prophecy of Malachi; but he also goes on to recall the sacrifices reaching back to "the beginning," to Abel in the Book of Genesis. In the Eucharist, Christ offers himself under appearances similar to those of the old sacrifices: bread and wine, the first-fruits of the earth. In the Eucharist, Christians "receive these antitypes," now made Christ's Body and Blood.

Furthermore, the Eucharist is the pledge of the resurrection of the body. Against the Gnostics, Irenaeus thunders:

> How can they say that the flesh, which is nourished with the body of the Lord and with his blood, goes to corruption? . . . For the bread, which is produced from the earth, is no longer common bread, once it has received the invocation of God; it is then the Eucharist, consisting of two realities, earthly and heavenly. So also our bodies, when they receive the Eucharist, are no longer corruptible, but have the hope of the resurrection to eternity.
>
> — *AGAINST HERESIES* 4.18.5

Finally, for Irenaeus, the Mass is the earthly participation in the liturgy of heaven, which is unveiled in the Book of Revelation. The altar of the Church and the altar of heaven are one (ibid. 4.18.6; cf. Rev 8:3-4; 11:1; 14:18).

For Irenaeus, the Christian "way of thinking is attuned to the Eucharist, and the Eucharist confirms our way of thinking" (*Against Heresies* 4.18.5). The later Fathers would recognize that principle at work and rephrase it as "*lex orandi, lex credendi*" — the law of prayer is the law of belief.

As that law worked to build up the Catholic Church, its violation brought about the destruction of the heretics. Irenaeus noted that the sectarians' missteps in doctrine often emerged as irregularities in liturgy as well. The Ebionites rejected the two natures of Jesus, divine and human, and held that Jesus was only human. So they refused to offer a mixed cup of wine and water — for the Church saw the mixed cup as a symbol of the god-man. In clear contradiction to Jesus' model and command, the Ebionites offered only water in their eucharistic chalice (*Against Heresies* 5.1.3). Marcion, for his part, held on to the Church's liturgy; but, in doing so, he committed himself to doctrinal inconsistency, for the Lord took bread and wine — things of creation, which Marcionite doctrine rejected as evil — and affirmed them to be his own sacred body and blood (*Against Heresies* 4.33.2).

The lesson in Irenaeus is clear: Those who tampered the Church's doctrine inevitably butchered the liturgy as well. And, in doing so, they cut themselves off from the ordinary means of salvation, the sacraments instituted by Christ himself.

The following passages are adapted from the 1892 Edinburgh edition of the Fathers.

On Sacrifice

[Jesus] directed his disciples to offer God the first-fruits of his own created things — not that he stood in need of gifts, but that the disciples might be neither unfruitful nor ungrateful. He took a created thing, bread, and gave thanks, and said, "This is my body" (Mt 26:26). And, likewise, the cup, which is part of the creation to which we belong, he confessed to be his blood.

Thus, he taught the new oblation of the new covenant, which the Church has received from the apostles and offers to God throughout all the world. For, in the New Testament, God provides, for our sustenance, the first-fruits of his own gifts. Malachi, among the twelve prophets, foretold this: "I will not accept an offering from your hand. For from the rising of the sun to its setting my name is great among the nations, and in every place incense is offered to my name, and a pure offering; for my name is great among the nations, says the Lord of hosts" (Mal 1:10-12). By these words he indicated in the plainest way that the former people [the Jews] shall cease to make offerings to God, but that everywhere a pure sacrifice shall be offered to him, and his name glorified among the Gentiles.

Now, what other name is glorified among the Gentiles but the Lord's, by which the Father is glorified, and man, too? Because it is the name of his own Son — who was made man by him — he calls it his own. A king who paints a likeness of his son is right to call this likeness his own, because it is [the likeness] of his son, and because it is his own work. So, too, does the Father confess the name of Jesus Christ — which is glorified by the Church throughout all the world — to be his own, both because it belongs to his Son and because he himself gave Jesus Christ for the salvation of men.

Thus, since the name of the Son belongs to the Father, and since in almighty God the Church makes offerings through Jesus Christ, he says rightly, "and in every place incense is offered to my name, and a pure offering" (Mal 1:11). In the Book of Revelation, John declares that the "incense" is "the prayers of the saints" (Rev 5:8).

The oblation of the Church is judged by God to be a pure and acceptable sacrifice. The Lord gave instructions that it should be offered throughout the world. He has no need of our sacrifice, but the one who offers is himself glorified in what he offers, if his gift is accepted. For the gift shows honor and affection toward the King; and the Lord himself, wishing us to offer it in all simplicity and innocence, said: "So if you are offering your gift at the altar, and there remember that your brother has something against you, leave your gift there before the altar and go; first be reconciled to your brother, and then come and offer your gift" (Mt 5:23-24).

First-fruits

We are bound, therefore, to offer God the first-fruits of his creation. Moses says, you "shall not appear before the Lord empty-handed" (Deut 16:16). Thus, man's acts of gratitude may show him to be grateful, and he may receive the honor that flows from God.

Oblations in general have not been set aside. For there were oblations there [among the Jews], and there are oblations here [among Christians]. There were sacrifices among the people; there are sacrifices, too, in the Church. Only the category has changed. Now the offering is made, not by slaves but by freemen. For the Lord is ever one and the same; but the character of a servile oblation is unique, as is that of freemen. Thus, the oblations themselves bear the mark of freedom. For with him there is nothing that lacks purpose, significance, or design. For this reason, they [the Jews] consecrated a tenth of their goods to him, but those who have received liberty set aside all their possessions for the Lord's purposes. They give joyfully and freely the more valuable portions of their property, since they have the hope of better things hereafter, like that poor widow who cast all her living into the treasury of God.

In the beginning, God respected the gifts of Abel, because he offered with single-mindedness and righteousness. But he had no respect for the offering of Cain, whose heart was divided by the envy and malice he held against his brother. As God said when reproving his hidden thoughts, "If you offer rightly, but do not divide rightly, have you not sinned? Be at rest" (Gen 4:7, *Septuagint*). For God is not appeased by sacrifice. What if someone should try to offer sacrifice merely by outward appearance — routinely, in due order, and according to the rules — while inwardly he does not give proper and rightful fellowship to his neighbor or due reverence to God?

He who cherishes secret sin in this way does not deceive God by a sacrifice offered correctly in outward appearance. Nor will such an oblation gain him anything if he does not give up the evil he harbors within — the sin that, through his hypocritical action, makes him his own murderer.

Thus did the Lord declare: "Woe to you, scribes and Pharisees, hypocrites! for you are like whitewashed tombs, which outwardly appear beautiful, but within they are full of dead men's bones and all uncleanness. So you also outwardly appear righteous to men, but within you are full of hypocrisy and iniquity" (Mt 23:27-28). While they appeared outwardly to offer correctly, they had jealousy inside, like Cain's; therefore they killed the Just One, slighting the counsel of the Word, as Cain did, too. For God said to him, "Be at rest," but he did not obey. Now what else does it mean to "be at rest" than to forego violence?

Saying similar things to these men, he declares: "You blind Pharisee! first cleanse the inside of the cup and of the plate, that the outside also may be clean" (Mt 23:26). But they did not listen to him. For Jeremiah says, "But you have eyes and heart only for your dishonest gain, for shedding innocent blood, and for practicing oppression and violence" (Jer 22:17). And Isaiah says, "[They] carry out a plan, but not mine; and make a league, but not of my spirit" (Is 30:1).

But God brought their inner wish and thought into the light to show that he is himself without blame and does no evil. When Cain was by no means at rest, God said to him: Sin's "desire is for you, but you must master it" (Gen 4:7). He spoke the same way to Pilate: "You would have no power over me unless it had been given you from above" (Jn 19:11).

God gives up the righteous one to suffering, so that, having been tested by what he suffered and endured, he may be accepted; but that the evildoer may be rejected, judged by the works he has done. Sacrifices, therefore, do not sanctify a man, for God stands in no need of sacrifice; it is, rather, the conscience of the offerer that makes the sacrifice holy when it is pure, and thus moves God to accept the offering as from a friend. "The sinner," he says, "who kills a calf in sacrifice to me, is as if he killed a dog" (see Is 66:3).

Since the Church offers with a pure heart, God justly judges that her sacrifice is pure. As Paul says to the Philippians, "I have received full payment, and more; I am filled, having received from Epaphroditus the gifts you sent, a fragrant offering, a sacrifice acceptable and pleasing to God" (4:18).

For it is our duty to make an oblation to God, and always to be grateful to God our Maker. We should offer the first-fruits of his own creation with a pure mind, and in faith without hypocrisy, in well-grounded hope, in fervent love. The Church alone offers this pure oblation to the Creator, offering him, with thanks, the things taken from his creation.

The Jews, however, do not make such offerings: for their "hands are full of blood" (Is 1:15); for they have not received the Word, who is offered to God. Nor, again, do any of the assemblies of the heretics. For some hold that the Father is different from the Creator; so, when they offer him what belongs to creation, they portray him as covetous of another's property, and wanting what is not his own. Others hold that the things around us originated from apostasy, ignorance, and passion; thus, while offering God the fruits of ignorance, passion, and apostasy, they sin against their Father, subjecting him to insult instead of giving him thanks. How can they be consistent when they say that the bread over which thanks have been given is the body of their Lord, and the cup his blood, if they do not call him the Son of the Creator of the world — that is, his Word, through whom the trees bear fruit, the fountains flow, and the earth gives "first the blade, then the ear, then the full grain in the ear" (Mk 4:28)?

Eucharist and Resurrection

Moreover, how can they say that the flesh, which is nourished with the body of the Lord and with his blood, goes to corruption, and does not partake of life?

Let them either change their opinion or stop offering the things just mentioned.

But our way of thinking is attuned to the Eucharist, and the Eucharist confirms our way of thinking. For we offer to him his own, announcing consistently the fellowship and union of the flesh and Spirit. For the bread, which is produced from the earth, is no longer common bread, once it has received the invocation of God; it is then the Eucharist, consisting of two realities, earthly and heavenly. So also our bodies, when they receive the Eucharist, are no longer corruptible, but have the hope of the resurrection to eternity.

We sacrifice to him, not as though he needed it, but giving thanks for his gift, and thus sanctifying what has been created. For even though God does not need our possessions, we do need to offer something to God. As Solomon said: "He who is kind to the poor lends to the Lord" (Prov 19:17). God, who stands in need of nothing, takes our good works to himself for this purpose: that he may reward us with his own good things. As our Lord said: "Come, O blessed of my Father, inherit the kingdom prepared for you from the foundation of the world; for I was hungry and you gave me food, I was thirsty and you gave me drink, I was a stranger and you welcomed me, I was naked and you clothed me, I was sick and you visited me, I was in prison and you came to me" (Mt 25:34-36). He does not stand in need of these services, yet he wants us to render them for our own benefit, lest we be unfruitful.

That is why the Word gave people that very precept regarding the making of oblations — although he stood in no need of them — that they might learn to serve God. It is his will that we, too, should offer a gift at the altar, frequently and without intermission. The altar, then, is in heaven, for toward that place are our prayers and oblations directed. The temple, too, is there. As John said in the Book of Revelation, "Then God's temple in heaven was opened" (Rev 11:19) along with the tabernacle: "Behold," He says, "the tabernacle of God, in which he will dwell with men" (Rev 21:3).

— *Against Heresies* 4.17.5-4.18.6

The Folly of Heresy

By shedding his true blood for us, and showing us his true flesh in the Eucharist, he conferred upon our flesh the capacity of salvation . . . Thus, those who despise the entire dispensation of God are fools. They disallow the salvation of the flesh, and treat its regeneration with contempt, maintaining that it is not capable of incorruption. But if flesh does not attain salvation, then neither did the Lord redeem us with his blood. Nor is the cup of the Eucharist the communion of his blood, nor the bread which we break the communion of his body. For blood can only come from veins and flesh and whatever else makes up the substance of man. And the Word of God was actually made flesh. By his own blood he redeemed us — as his apostle declares, "In whom we have redemption through his blood, the remission of sins" (see Col 1:14).

As we are his members, we are also nourished by means of the creation. He himself grants us the creation, for he causes his sun to rise and sends rain when he wills. He has acknowledged the cup, which is a part of creation, as his own blood, from which he bedews our blood; and he has established the bread, also a part of creation, as his own body, from which he gives increase to our bodies. When the mingled cup and the man-made bread receive the Word of God, they become the Eucharist of the blood and the body of Christ. From these things the substance of our flesh is increased and supported.

How, then, can they affirm that the flesh is incapable of receiving the gift of God, which is life eternal? This flesh is nourished from the body and blood of the Lord, and is a member of him! As St. Paul declares in his Epistle to the Ephesians: "We are members of his body" (Eph 5:30), of his flesh and bones. He is not talking about some spiritual and invisible man, for a spirit does not have bones or flesh. He is talking about that dispensation by which the Lord became an actual man, consisting of flesh, nerves, and bones — flesh that is nourished by the cup which is his blood, and receives increase from the bread which is his body.

A cutting from the vine planted in the ground bears fruit in its season. A grain of wheat falls into the earth and decomposes, before rising in abundance by the Spirit of God, who contains all things. It is then that this wheat, through the wisdom of God, becomes useful for men; and, after receiving the Word of God, it becomes the Eucharist, the body and blood of Christ.

In the same way, our bodies, which are nourished by the Eucharist, are buried in the earth and decompose. Yet they shall rise at their appointed time, when the Word of God grants them resurrection to the glory of God. The Father freely gives immortality to the mortal, and incorruption to the corruptible, because the strength of God is made perfect in weakness, in order that we may never become puffed up and ungrateful, thinking that we have life from ourselves and that we are exalted over God.

We must learn by experience that we have eternal duration, not by our own nature but from the excellent power of this Being. And we must never undervalue the glory that surrounds God as he is, nor be ignorant of our own nature. Knowing what God can do and what benefits man receives, we must never wander from true understanding of things as they are — with regard to God and with regard to man. Might it not be the case, as I have already observed, that this is why God permitted us to be dissolved into the common dust of mortality: that, after learning by every mode, we may be accurate in all things for the future, ignorant neither of God nor of ourselves?

— *AGAINST HERESIES* 5.2.1-3

Not Carnal, But Spiritual Worship

Those who have become acquainted with the secondary constitutions of the apostles are aware that the Lord instituted a new oblation in the new covenant, according to Malachi the prophet: "From the rising of the sun to its setting my name is great among the nations, and in every place incense is offered to my name, and a pure offering" (Mal 1:11). John, too, declared in the Book of Revelation: "The incense is the prayers of the saints" (Rev 5:8). Then again, Paul exhorts us: "Present your bodies as a living sacrifice, holy and acceptable to God, which is your spiritual worship" (Rom 12:1). And again: "Let us offer up a sacrifice of praise to God, that is, the fruit of the lips" (Heb 13:15).

Now those oblations are not according to the law, whose written expression the Lord took away and canceled. Rather, they are according to the Spirit, for we must worship God "in spirit and in truth" (Jn 4:24).

Thus, the oblation of the Eucharist is not carnal, but spiritual; and in this respect it is pure. For we make an oblation to God of the bread and the cup of blessing, giving him thanks that he has commanded the earth to bring forth these fruits for our nourishment. Then, when we have perfected the oblation, we invoke the Holy Spirit, that he may present this sacrifice — both the bread, the body of Christ; and the cup, the blood of Christ — so that those who receive these antitypes may also receive remission of sins and eternal life. Those, then, who perform these oblations in remembrance of the Lord do not fall in with Jewish views. Performing the service in a spiritual way, they shall be called children of wisdom.

— FRAGMENT OF A LOST WORK

The False Rites of a Charlatan

Among the heretics, there is a certain Marcus. . . . An expert in magical illusions, he uses these as a means of drawing away many men and not a few women. He entices them to join him, as one who holds the greatest knowledge and perfection and has received the highest power from the invisible and ineffable regions above. Thus, he appears as if he really were the precursor of Antichrist. For, joining the buffooneries of Anaxilaus to the craftiness of the magicians, he is regarded by his senseless and cracked-brain followers as working miracles by these means.

Pretending to consecrate cups mixed with wine, and stretching the word of invocation to great length, he contrives to give the contents a purple and reddish color. Charis, who [according to Marcus's teaching] is one of those that are superior to all things, is alleged to drop her own blood into that cup through means of his invocation. Those who are present are supposed to rejoice to taste from that cup, because, by so doing, the Charis, who is set forth by this magician, may also flow into them.

Again, handing mixed cups to the women, he bids them to consecrate these in his presence. When this has been done, he himself produces another cup, of much larger size than that which the deluded woman had consecrated. Pouring from the smaller one consecrated by the woman into the one that he has brought forward, he pronounces these words: "May that Charis who is before all things, and who transcends all knowledge and speech, fill your inner man, and multiply in you her own knowledge, by sowing the grain of mustard seed in you as in good soil." Repeating other, similar words, and thus goading on the wretched woman [to madness], he then appears a worker of miracles when the large cup is seen to have been filled from the small one, and even to overflow with what has been obtained from it.

By accomplishing such things, he has completely deceived many, and drawn them away after him.

— *Against Heresies* 1.13.1-2

CHAPTER 13

St. Hippolytus of Rome

An early manual of Church regulations, the *Apostolic Tradition* of Hippolytus, offers us perhaps the most complete liturgy that has survived from the first two centuries. The circumstances and nature of this liturgy, however, are difficult to determine. Some believe it was the standard rite used in the Church of Rome in the first centuries (Dix 1945:157; Jungmann 1959:54; Deiss 1979:126). Others say that it was an Eastern liturgy mistakenly attributed to a Roman writer. Still others conclude that it was never actually used as a liturgy, but was rather an idealized rite (Bouyer 1968:165) concocted by a would-be reformer — a schismatic pretender to the papacy.

A great part of the problem is that the full text of the *Apostolic Tradition* has not survived. The work is known only through later editions, some in translation from the original Greek, that were extensively revised, expanded, and adapted to local custom. Comparing these various editions to one another and to quotations in other works of the Fathers, several modern scholars have attempted to reconstruct the original text.

Controversy has likely surrounded the *Apostolic Tradition* since it was written in 215. If, indeed, it was written by Hippolytus — and scholars do dispute this — then it was a product of the first antipope. Hippolytus was a Greek-speaking priest, perhaps from Egypt, serving in Rome during the late second and early third centuries. Early histories tell us that he was a disciple of Irenaeus.

A noted theologian in his day, Hippolytus thought that Pope Callixtus I (217-222) had invalidated his authority by excessive leniency toward heretics, and so Hippolytus had himself elected "pope" by a group of influential Roman priests. He extended his claim through the reign of three legitimate popes. In 235, the imperial authorities sentenced both Hippolytus and the recently resigned Pope Pontian to exile on the island of Sardinia. Hippolytus was reconciled with the Church before dying for his faith, along with Pontian. Their bodies were transferred together to Rome for burial. It seems that the Church venerated him almost immediately. A third-century monument honors him with an allegorical representation of wisdom and a full listing of his many literary works, including the *Apostolic Tradition*.

The *Apostolic Tradition* is valuable because it contains a complete eucharistic prayer, as well as the introductory dialogue that still remains in the Western liturgy: "The Lord be with you. And with your spirit. Lift up your hearts. We lift them up to the Lord." Hippolytus also gives us a glimpse of liturgical traditions that vanished long ago — for example, the custom of dispensing a chalice of milk and honey, along with the eucharistic elements, during the Easter liturgy. This symbolized the newly baptized Christian's entrance into the true promised land through the sacraments. (The chalice of milk and honey is attested to by many other authors as well, including pseudo-Barnabas, Tertullian, Ambrose, and Jerome. See Danielou 1964:333-334.)

The *Apostolic Tradition* provides an important early witness to the enduring Real Presence of Jesus in the Eucharist. Hippolytus counsels his readers to take special care with the reserved sacrament, "for it is the body of Christ to be consumed by those who believe and not to be treated lightly." He also urges Christians not to spill even a drop from the chalice of Christ's Blood. This idea is implicit in earlier texts that speak of the deacons taking the sacrament to the sick who are homebound, but Hippolytus' discussion shows, perhaps, the Church's growing pastoral concern for reverence toward the Eucharist.

Compared to his predecessors in the documentary trail, Hippolytus seems almost cavalier in setting down the prayers and doctrine of the Mass, along with detailed practical advice. Yet he acknowledges the discipline of the secret and exhorts Christians to "let not unbelievers know [these teachings] until they are baptized. This is the white stone of which John said: 'I will give him a white stone, with a new name written on the stone which no one knows except him who receives the stone' " (Rev 2:17).

The eucharistic prayer of the *Apostolic Tradition* is embedded in the rite of ordination for a bishop. The text is dense with scriptural allusions from both the Old and New Testaments. Indeed, almost every phrase derives from the Bible.

The *Apostolic Tradition* was enormously influential in the Church's liturgical movement throughout the twentieth century. Catholics will recognize Hippolytus' eucharistic prayer as the foundation for Eucharistic Prayer II.

In his works of Scripture scholarship, Hippolytus discerned that the Eucharist was the earthly participation in the heavenly banquet, foreshadowed even in the Old Testament.

Readers interested in the textual difficulties in studying Hippolytus will find a fascinating summary in *The Study of Liturgy* (Jones et al. 1992:87-88, 213-216).

The following translation is new, but dependent in parts upon the work of Burton Scott Easton (1934) and Gregory Dix (1937). The fragment from the *Commentary on Proverbs* is based on the translation in the Edinburgh edition of the Fathers (1892).

The Eucharistic Prayer

Bishop: The Lord be with you.

And all shall say: And with your spirit.

Bishop: Lift up your hearts.

All: We lift them up to the Lord.

Bishop: Let us give thanks to the Lord.

All: It is proper and right.

Bishop: We give you thanks, O God, through your beloved Child Jesus Christ, whom you have sent us in these last days as Savior, Redeemer, and Messenger of your counsel. He is your Word, inseparable from you, through whom you created all things and in whom you are well pleased. From heaven you sent him into the womb of the Virgin, and, once conceived within her, he was made flesh, and was shown to be your Son, born of the Holy Spirit and the Virgin. Fulfilling your will and winning for you a holy people, he stretched out his hands as he suffered, that by his death he might free those who believed in you.

When he was betrayed to his willing death, so that he might abolish death, break the bonds of the devil, trample hell under foot, give light to the righteous, set a term of sentence, and manifest his resurrection, he took bread and, giving thanks to you, said: "Take, eat: This is my body, which is broken for you."

In the same way, the cup, saying: "This is my blood, which is shed for you. When you do this, do so in memory of me."

And so, keeping in mind his death and resurrection, we offer you the bread and the cup, giving thanks because you have counted us worthy to stand before you and serve you.

We pray that you would send your Holy Spirit upon the offerings of your holy Church. Gathering them together, grant that all your saints who partake may be filled with the Holy Spirit, that their faith may be confirmed in truth, that we may praise you and give you glory, through your Child Jesus Christ, through whom be glory and honor, with the Holy Spirit in the holy Church, now and for ever. Amen.

— *APOSTOLIC TRADITION*

At Easter Mass

The deacons immediately bring the offering to the bishop, who, by giving thanks, shall make the bread into an antitype of the body of Christ, and the cup of wine mixed with water into the likeness of his blood, which is shed for all who believe in him. Milk and honey shall be mixed together in fulfillment of the promise given to the patriarchs, of a land flowing with milk and honey. This is Christ's flesh, which he gave, by which those who believe are nourished like babies. He sweetens the bitterness of the heart by the gentleness of his word. Water is brought as a sign of the washing, in order that the inner part of man, which is spiritual, may receive the same as the body. The bishop shall explain the reason for all these things to those who partake. And when he breaks the bread and distributes the fragments he shall say: "The heavenly bread in Christ Jesus." And the recipient shall say, "Amen."

The priests — or if there are not enough priests, the deacons — shall hold the cups, and stand with reverence and dignity; first the one who holds the water, next the milk, then the wine. The recipients shall taste three times from each. He who gives the cup shall say: "In God the Father Almighty." And the recipient shall say, "Amen." Then: "In the Lord Jesus Christ." And he shall say, "Amen." Then: "In the Holy Ghost and holy Church." And he shall say, "Amen." So it shall be done to each. And when these things are completed, let each hasten to do good and please God and live rightly, devoting himself to the Church, practicing what he has learned, advancing in the service of God.

— *Apostolic Tradition*

Care for the Eucharist

Let everyone take care that no unbaptized person taste the Eucharist, nor a mouse or other animal, and that none of it fall and be lost. For it is the body of Christ to be consumed by those who believe and not to be treated lightly.

After the cup has been blessed in the name of God, you receive it as the antitype of the blood of Christ. So spill nothing from it. May no strange spirit lap it up because you despised it and rendered yourself guilty of the blood of Christ — like a man who despises the price with which he has been ransomed.

— *Apostolic Tradition*

Wisdom's Banquet

"Wisdom has built her house, she has set up her seven pillars" (Prov 9:1). This means Christ, the wisdom and power of God the Father, has built his house, his nature in the flesh derived from the Virgin. It is just as John said: "And the Word became flesh and dwelt among us" (Jn 1:14). So the wise prophet also testifies: Wisdom that was before the world, and is the source of life, the infinite Wisdom of God, has built her house, by a mother who knew no man — that is, as he assumed the temple of the body.

"She has set up her seven pillars," and these are the fragrant grace of the all-holy Spirit, as Isaiah says: "And the seven spirits of God shall rest upon Him" (Is 11:2). But others say that the seven pillars are the seven divine orders that sustain creation by His holy and inspired teaching: the prophets, the apostles, the martyrs, the bishops, the hermits, the saints, and the righteous. . . .

The passage goes on to say, "she has mixed her wine, she has also set her table" (Prov 9:2). "She has mixed her wine" means that the Savior, uniting His Godhead, like pure wine, with the flesh in the Virgin, was born of her. He was simultaneously God and man, without confusion of the one in the other. "She has also set her table": This denotes the promised knowledge of the Holy Trinity; it also refers to his honored and undefiled body and blood, which day by day are administered and offered sacrificially at the spiritual divine table, as a memorial of that first and ever-memorable table of the spiritual divine supper.

It goes on: "She has sent out her maids." Wisdom has done so — Christ has done so — "to call from the highest places in the town, 'Whoever is simple, let him turn in here!'" So she says, in an obvious reference to the holy Apostles, who traveled the whole world, summoning the nations, with their lofty and divine preaching, to the knowledge of him in truth.

The passage continues, "To those who want under-standing she says" — to those, that is, who have not yet received the power of the Holy Spirit — "Come, eat of my bread and drink of the wine I have mixed." By this is meant that he gave his divine flesh and precious blood to us, to eat and to drink for the remission of sins.

— FRAGMENT ON PROVERBS

CHAPTER 14

The *Didascalia*

The *Didascalia Apostolorum* — in full, the *Catholic Teaching of the Twelve Holy Apostles and Disciples of Our Savior* — follows after the *Apostolic Tradition* of Hippolytus and the *Didache*. It is a "Church order" — that is, a manual of moral, liturgical, ascetical, and ecclesiastical discipline and instruction.

Composed in Syria between the years 200 and 250, the *Didascalia* offers very practical advice for conduct during worship. As there is an order to the Church, so there is an order to the liturgy, and that arrangement is manifest even in small details, such as seating preferences and the direction of one's prayer (always eastward).

A distinct social order flows from this peaceable liturgy, where the poor and strangers are as welcome as the bishop: "If a poor man or woman comes to you . . . and there is no room, the deacon shall find a place for them, O bishop, even if you yourself must sit on the ground."

"Widows and orphans," the author says later, "should be revered like the altar."

The *Didascalia* offers a very early witness to the practice of offering Mass for the dead, urging Christians to "pray and offer for those who have fallen asleep." The author also mentions the early Christian practice, so evident in the catacombs, of offering Mass at gravesites.

The *Didascalia* profoundly influenced many subsequent Church orders. A century later, the Apostolic Constitutions, another Syrian document, would synthesize portions of the *Didascalia* along with the *Didache* and the *Apostolic Tradition*.

It was common for the early Church to attribute legislative texts to the apostles, since the law of the Church reflected the apostolic spirit, tradition, and authority.

The following passages of the *Didascalia* have been extracted and adapted from the Edinburgh edition of the Apostolic Constitutions. R.H. Connolly has produced a complete translation of the Syriac text.

Order in the Church

When you call an assembly of the Church, conduct your meetings in an exemplary way. Set places for the brethren with all due care and decency. Keep a place for the priests in the east end of the house. In the middle let the bishop's throne be placed, and on each side of him let the priests sit down. Laymen should fill the remaining space in the east end of the house. It is right for the priests to be placed first with the bishops in the east end of the house, then the laymen, then the women, so that, when you stand for prayer, the presiders may stand first, followed by the laymen and the women. Pray facing the east, for it is written: Give thanks to God who rides on the eastern side of the highest heavens.

As to the deacons, let one of them attend upon the oblation of the Eucharist, another stand outside at the door, minding those who enter. If anyone should be found sitting out of his place, let him be rebuked by the deacon and moved into the place proper for him. . . .

Let young people sit by themselves, if there is space for them; if not, let them stand. Let those who are already stricken in years sit in order. Children should stand aside, or let their fathers and mothers take them and remain standing with them. Let the younger women also sit by themselves, if there is space for them; but if there is not, let them stand behind the women. Let those women who are married with children be placed by themselves, but let the widows and older women sit by themselves.

Let the deacon be in charge of the places, that everyone who comes in may go to his proper place and nowhere else. In the same way, let the deacon supervise the people, so that nobody may whisper, nor slumber, nor laugh, nor nod; for in church everyone should stand with dignity, attentive to the word of the Lord.

If any brother, man or woman, comes in from another parish, let the deacon inquire as to whether they are married or widowed, a child of the Church or a heretic. Then he may lead them to be seated in the proper place.

If a priest comes from another parish, let him be received by the priests into their place. If he is a bishop, let him sit with the bishop and be accorded the same honor and the same place. And you, O bishop, should invite him to speak to the people words of instruction: for the exhortation and admonition of strangers are exceedingly useful.

If a poor man or woman comes to you, whether from your parish or not, but especially if they are old, and there is no room, the deacon shall find a place for them, O bishop, even if you yourself must sit on the ground. You must not make distinctions between persons, if you want your service to please God. . . .

When you teach the people, O bishop, command and exhort them to come faithfully to church, and never forsake it for any reason, but gather together continually. Let no one diminish the Church by withdrawing themselves. If they do, they deprive the body of Christ of one of its members.

CHAPTER 15

Sts. Abercius and Pectorius

The "discipline of the secret" was the respectful silence the early Christians observed in regard to the mysteries of faith. When alluding to the sacraments in their homilies and commentaries, bishops and teachers would usually shift to a sort of code — a symbolic language dense with scriptural allusions, understandable only to someone living a deeply Christian life.

This code extended beyond literary work and preaching, to paintings, sculpture, epitaphs, and even graffiti. In the catacombs of Callixtus in Rome, carvings evoke the sacraments through symbols. Christ was the fish, because the initials of his name, "Jesus Christ, Son of God, Savior," spelled *ichthos*, the Greek word for fish. Pictorial symbols of the Eucharist were many: a bird pecking at grapes symbolized the soul drawing nourishment from the sacrament; a banquet of fish, bread, and wine suggested at once the eucharistic liturgy and Jesus' multiplication of loaves and fishes.

Burial inscriptions — given their limited space — tended to condense this language to an even greater degree, so that they convey little more than a cryptic catalog of images. Two ancient epitaphs, those of Sts. Abercius and Pectorius, offer good examples.

The inscription of Abercius dates to 216 or earlier. The bishop of Hieropolis in Phrygia (now part of Turkey), Abercius made a pilgrimage to Rome during a period of relative peace for Christians. While there, he wrote his own epitaph. While clear to Abercius' fellow believers, the twenty-two lines of metered Greek would surely baffle the uninitiated. Christ appears as the fish and the shepherd; the Church of Rome is represented as a queen dressed in gold; the Blessed Virgin Mary is "the chaste virgin"; the mass of believers are a "people marked with a sign" — the sign of the cross.

The text of the epitaph was published widely in the biographies of Abercius and was adopted by later Christians who merely substituted their own names for that of Abercius. Abercius' original burial marker now stands in the Lateran Museum in Rome.

The Latin inscription of Pectorius was unearthed in Autun, France. Its age is uncertain, but its style corresponds to that of Abercius, using similarly cryptic language to describe the Eucharist.

The Inscription of Abercius

A citizen of the chosen city, I made this [tomb] in my lifetime, so that I might have a resting place for my body. My name is Abercius, and I am a disciple of the chaste shepherd, who feeds his flock of sheep on the mountains and in the meadows. His eyes are large, seeing everywhere. He taught me from the faithful writings.

He sent me to Rome, to contemplate his kingdom and to see a queen with golden robe and golden sandals. There I saw a renowned people marked by a splendid sign. And I saw all the plains and cities of Syria, even Nisibis. Having crossed the Euphrates, I traveled everywhere with Paul as a companion.

Faith then was my guide, and set before me as nourishment the fish from the deep: very large, very pure, this fish that the chaste virgin held in her arms; that she gave to its friends to eat everywhere, having excellent wine, giving it as a drink mixed with water, together with bread.

These words Abercius dictated while standing nearby and ordered them to be inscribed here during the seventy-second year of his life. Let everyone who understands these things and grasps their meaning pray for Abercius. Let no man place another in my tomb unless he pays two thousand gold pieces to the treasury of the Romans, and a thousand gold pieces to my beloved fatherland Hieropolis.

The Inscription of Pectorius

O divine race of the heavenly fish, with a respectful heart receive immortal life among mortals. Rejuvenate your soul, my friend, in divine waters, by wisdom's eternal streams, which give true riches. Receive the delicious nourishment of the Savior of the saints. Eat, drink, taking the fish with both hands.

CHAPTER 16

Apocryphal and Heretical Texts

The books of the early Church included what Justin called the "memoirs of the apostles": the Gospels, Acts, and letters of the men Jesus had chosen. These are the books that were canonized, or approved for use in the liturgy.

But the books we know today as the New Testament were not the only ones claiming authority in ancient times. Wherever the Church spread, there would arise a brisk industry in what we now call apocryphal gospels, acts, and epistles. Many of these texts have survived the centuries and even influenced popular piety. They vary widely in their orthodoxy, historical accuracy, and literary quality. Most are fanciful fictions; some adapt pagan myths and folktales to Christian purposes; still others use the biblical characters as mere mouthpieces for the authors' aberrant theology or metaphysical system. What they all have in common is that the Church rejected them as inauthentic and uninspired.

Yet even these are valuable for what they show us (as through a glass, darkly) about the eucharistic practice of the primitive Church.

Most of the passages below have been adapted from the 1892 Edinburgh edition of the Fathers. The selection from the *Acts of Peter* is adapted from M.R. James' *The Apocryphal New Testament* (Oxford: Clarendon, 1924). The *Gospel of Judas* is available in both Coptic transcription and English translation on the website of the National Geographic Society; the passage below is prepared from those editions.

The Last Eucharist of John

The earliest of the apocryphal documents that discuss the Eucharist, the *Acts of John* may have been written in Asia Minor around the year 150. Blatantly Gnostic in doctrine, Pseudo-John describes Jesus' body as unreal and immaterial, and his suffering and death as illusions. The Acts describes several eucharistic liturgies that appear to use bread alone or, perhaps, bread and water. This could be further evidence of the Acts' heretical origin, as many Gnostic sects practiced a severe discipline that forbade the use of wine, even in worship. Though Pseudo-John refers to the Lord's "body and blood," the text refers only to bread and never to wine. In a passage not included here, the *Acts of John* provides a very early witness of the Church's practice of offering Mass at the graves of martyrs.

> What was his end like, and how did he depart from men? On the following day, which was the Lord's day, and in the presence of the brethren, he began to say to them: "Brethren, fellow servants, co-heirs, and co-partners of the kingdom of the Lord, consider the miracles the Lord has shown you through me. What wonders, cures, signs, favors, teachings, rulings, rests, services, glories, graces, gifts, faiths, communions — things that ear has not heard, you have seen with your eyes. Be strong, therefore, in him, remembering him in all you do, knowing the mystery of the dispensation that has come to men, for the sake of which the Lord has worked. . . ."

Then he asked for bread and gave thanks, saying: "What praise, or what sort of offering, or what thanksgiving, shall we invoke, breaking the bread, but only you? We glorify the name by which the Father has called you. We glorify the name by which you have been called through the Son. We glorify the resurrection which has been manifested to us through you. Of you we glorify the seed, the word, the grace, the true pearl, the treasure, the plow, the net, the majesty, the crown, him who is called Son of man for our sakes, the truth, the rest, the knowledge, the freedom, the place of refuge in you. For you alone are Lord, the root of immortality, the fountain of incorruption, and the seat of the ages; you who have been called all these for our sakes, that now we, calling upon you through these, may recognize your illimitable majesty, shown by your presence, that can be seen only by the pure, seen in your only Son."

After breaking the bread, he gave it to us, praying for each of the brethren, that he might be worthy of the Eucharist of the Lord. He also tasted it, saying: "To me also let there be a portion with you, and peace, O beloved." After saying this, he confirmed the brethren. Then he said to Eutyches, also named Verus: "Behold, I appoint you a minister of the Church of Christ, and I entrust you with the flock of Christ. Be mindful, therefore, of the commandments of the Lord; and if you should fall into trials or dangers, do not be afraid; for you shall face many troubles, and you shall be proven an eminent witness of the Lord. Thus, Verus, attend to the flock as a servant of God until the time appointed for your testimony."

— *ACTS OF JOHN*

For Compassion, Mercy, Reward

Like the *Acts of John*, the Syriac *Acts of Thomas,* probably composed in the third century, never mentions a chalice of wine. In
its liturgical scenes, however, Thomas employs Trinitarian formulas and even describes a sinner suffering bodily harm upon taking
the Eucharist — both unusual in Gnostic texts. Typical of Gnostic
texts, however, Thomas takes a dim view of marriage and even
exhorts spouses to separate.

> He continued in his fasting, for the Lord's day was
> about to dawn. And on the night following, while he
> was asleep, the Lord came and stood by his head, saying:
> "Thomas, rise up early and bless them all; and after the
> prayer and service go along the eastern road two miles,
> and there I shall show in you my glory. For because you
> go away, many shall flee to me for refuge, and you shall
> reprove the nature and the power of the enemy."
>
> Rising from sleep, he said to the brethren who were
> with him: "Children and brethren, the Lord wishes to do
> something today through me. Let us pray and beg him
> that nothing may hinder us toward him, but let it now,
> as always, be done unto us according to his purpose and
> will." After speaking, he laid his hands upon them and
> blessed them. And breaking the bread of the Eucha-
> rist, he gave it to them, saying: "This Eucharist shall be
> to you for compassion, mercy, and reward, and not for
> judgment." And they said: "Amen."
>
> — *ACTS OF THOMAS*

A Murderer Takes the Sacrament

After laying his hands on them, he blessed them, saying: "The grace of our Lord Jesus Christ be upon you for ever!" And they said, "Amen." And a woman begged of him, saying: "Apostle of the Most High, give me the seal, that that foe may not come back upon me again." Then he made her come near him; and putting his hand upon her, he sealed her in the name of Father, and Son, and Holy Spirit. And many others also were sealed along with her.

Then the apostle ordered his servant to set a table; and they set up a bench that they found there. Spreading a linen cloth upon it, he placed on it the bread of the blessing. The apostle stood by it and said: "Jesus Christ, Son of God, you have deemed us worthy of communion with the Eucharist of your sacred body and honorable blood. See, we are made bold by the thanksgiving and invocation of your sacred name. Come now, and communicate with us." And he began to say: "Come, perfect compassion; come, communion with mankind; come, you who know the mysteries of the chosen one; come, you who participate in all the combats of the noble warrior; come, peace that reveals the great things of all greatness; come, you who disclose secrets, and reveal things not to be spoken; the sacred dove that has brought forth twin young; come, you secret mother; come, you who are manifest in your deeds, and give joy and rest to those who are united to you; come and commune with us in this Eucharist, which we make in the name, and in the love in which we are united in calling upon you."

Then he made the sign of the cross upon the bread, and broke it, and began to distribute it. And first he gave it to the woman, saying: "This shall be for remission of your sins, and the ransom of everlasting transgressions." Afterward, he gave also to all the others who had received the seal.

There was a certain young man who had done a nefarious deed. Coming to the apostle, he took the bread of the Eucharist into his mouth, and his two hands immediately withered, so that he could no longer bring them to his mouth. Those who were there and saw him told the apostle what had happened. He summoned him and said: "Tell me, my child, and be ashamed of nothing, what you have done and why you have come here; for the Eucharist of the Lord has convicted you. This gracious gift comes to many and is especially healing to those who approach it through faith and love. But it has withered you away, and there must be some reason for this."

The young man who had been convicted by the Eucharist of the Lord came up and fell at the apostle's feet, and begged him, saying: "An evil deed has been done by me, yet I thought to do something good. I was in love with a certain woman living outside of the city in an inn, and she loved me. And I, after hearing you, believed that you proclaim the living God. So I came and received the seal from you along with the others; and you said, 'Whoever shall indulge in filthy intercourse, and especially in adultery, shall not have life with the God whom I proclaim.' Since, then, I altogether loved her, I begged and pleaded with her to live with me in chaste and pure companionship, as you teach. But she would not. When she would not, I took a sword and killed her, for I could not see her living in adultery with another."

— *ACTS OF THOMAS*

Establishing a Church

The *Acts of Thaddeus* is a product of third-century Syria. Though doctrinally more orthodox than Thomas and John, Thaddeus is rather ambitious in its historical fictions, which include purported correspondence between Jesus and the king of Edessa. It is valuable, however, for its description of the sacraments of initiation, and for revealing what was important in the establishment of a new Church: the ordination of clergy who were carefully instructed in, among other things, the conduct of the liturgy. The Thaddeus who is the subject of these Acts was purported to be one of Jesus' original seventy-two disciples and the author of the *Liturgy of Addai [Thaddeus] and Mari,* which could be the rite of ancient Edessa.

After the passion, resurrection, and ascension, Thaddeus went to Abgar [a king who had been healed by the word of Jesus]. Finding him in health, he gave him an account of the incarnation of Christ, and baptized him with all his house. Then, after instructing great multitudes, both of Hebrews and Greeks, Syrians and Armenians, he baptized them in the name of the Father, and Son, and Holy Spirit, having anointed them with the holy perfume; and he gave them communion with the undefiled mysteries of the sacred body and blood of our Lord Jesus Christ, and told them to keep and observe the law of Moses, and to heed closely the things that had been said by the apostles in Jerusalem. Year by year they came together to the Passover, and again he imparted to them the Holy Spirit.

And Thaddeus along with Abgar destroyed the temples of idols and built churches. He ordained as bishop one of his disciples, and priests and deacons, and taught them the rubrics of the psalmody and the holy liturgy.

— *Acts of Thaddeus*

Paul's Vision of Hell

The apocalyptic *Vision of Paul* is likely a product of Egypt, composed around 250. Its author reserves a special place in hell for those who abuse the liturgy.

I saw the fiery river and saw there a man being tortured by Tartaruchian angels having in their hands an iron with three hooks with which they pierced the bowels of that old man. And I asked the angel: "Sir, who is that old man on whom such torments are imposed?" And the angel answered: "He whom you see was a priest who did not perform well his ministry. When he had been eating and drinking and committing fornication, he offered the host to the Lord at his holy altar."

Then he carried me south and placed me above a well, and I found it sealed with seven seals. And the angel who was with me said to the angel of that place: "Open the mouth of the well so that Paul, the well-beloved of God, may see, for he has been authorized to see all the pains of hell." And the angel said to me: "Stand afar off so that you may be able to bear the stench of this place."

When the well was opened, immediately there arose a hard and wicked stench, which surpassed all punishments. I looked into the well and I saw fiery masses glowing in every part, and narrow places. The mouth of the well was narrow so as to admit only one man. And the angel said to me: "If any man is put into this well of the abyss and it is sealed over him, no remembrance of him shall ever be made in the sight of the Father and his Son and the holy angels.

I said: "Who are these, sir, who are put into this well?"

And he said to me: "They are whoever shall not confess that Christ has come in the flesh and that the Virgin Mary brought him forth, and whoever says that the bread and cup of the eucharistic blessing are not the body and blood of Christ."

— *THE VISION OF PAUL*

The Wages of Sin

The consequences of making a bad communion is a theme frequently treated in the apocrypha. The following story is typical. It from the second-century Greek *Acts of Peter*, in the seventh-century edition known as *The Vercelli Acts*.

They brought Paul bread and water for the sacrifice, so that he might pray and distribute it to everyone. A woman named Rufina wished to receive the Eucharist at the hands of Paul. Paul, filled with the spirit of God, said to her as she drew near: "Rufina, you do not come worthily to the altar of God. You rise up from beside an adulterer, a man who is not your husband, and you attempt to receive the Eucharist of God. Behold, Satan shall trouble your heart and cast you down in the sight of all those who believe in the Lord, so that those who see and believe may know that they have believed in the living God, the searcher of hearts. If you repent of your act, he is faithful and able to blot out your sin and set you free from this sin. But if you do not repent, the devouring fire and outer darkness shall receive you forever, while you are still in the body." Immediately, Rufina fell down, stricken with palsy from her head to her feet, and she had no power to speak, for her tongue was bound.

— *ACTS OF PETER* 2

A Reversal of Fortunes: The Gospel of Judas

The *Gospel of Judas* is mentioned briefly in Irenaeus's second-century refutation of the heresies. Its text, however, was lost for centuries — until its publication, with much fanfare, by the National Geographic Society at Easter in 2006. "Judas" represents the extreme fringe of Gnosticism's re-interpretation of Jesus. In this text, all Christian values are turned upside down. The heroes of the New Testament, Jesus' disciples, are declared anathema with all their spiritual offspring. The narrative opens with a portrayal of Jesus himself mocking orthodox Christianity's most sacred rite, the Mass.

One day he was with his disciples in Judea, and he found them assembled and seated in pious observance. When he approached his disciples, assembled and seated and offering the eucharistic prayer over the bread, he laughed.

The disciples said to him, "Master, why are you laughing at our eucharistic prayer? We have done what is right."

He replied and said to them, "I am not laughing at you. You do this not because of your own will, but because it is through this that your god will be praised."

They said, "Master, you are the son of our god."

Jesus said to them, "How do you know me? Truly I say to you, no generation of the people among you will know me."

When his disciples heard this, they began to get angry and furious and started blaspheming against him in their hearts.

When Jesus saw that they did not understand, he said to them, "Why has this agitation led you to anger? Your god who is within you provoked you to anger within your souls. Let any one of you who is strong enough among men bring out the perfect man and stand before my face."

They all said, "We have the strength."

But their spirits did not dare to stand before him, except for Judas Iscariot.

CHAPTER 17

Pagan Rumors

When Pliny the Younger insists that the Christians and their liturgy were harmless and ordinary, we may infer that some of his fellow citizens thought otherwise. Indeed, when he conducted his interrogations, Pliny may have been investigating charges of sexual debauchery, ritual murder, and cannibalism. These accusations were common in ancient anti-Christian polemics. Christian apologists such as Justin, Minucius Felix, and Tertullian covered yards of parchment in defense against such slanders.

Today the rumors seem ludicrous; but for the early Christians, they presented a clear and present danger. Lurid tales of wrongdoing could incite mobs, bring on new interrogations (usually aided by torture), or motivate governors to renew or intensify a persecution.

As early as the first or second century, a certain Lollianus wrote a fiction purporting to describe the child-murder ritually practiced by Christians in their liturgy. Marcus Cornelius Fronto (d. 166) recounted tales of Sunday worship that included drunken orgies and infanticide. A more measured intellectual, Celsus, writing around 185, said that Christians were guilty merely of practicing magic, which was itself a crime. His description of "priests [using] books containing magical formulas" probably refers to the liturgy.

Many of these charges likely arose from misunderstandings nurtured by bigotry. Christians called their ritual meal an agape, or "love feast"; to malicious ears, that suggested an orgy. Christian Scriptures spoke of eating the flesh of Christ and drinking his blood — and what could that be but cannibalism?

It is possible that some of the accusations were based on true stories about Christian heretical sects. While some Gnostic schools emphasized strict discipline, others encouraged licentious behavior, teaching that all the commandments of the demiurge Yahweh must be broken. This, of course, led to bizarre behavior, ranging from promiscuity to murder. Church Fathers, such as Epiphanius (*Panarion* 26.4-5) in the fourth century and John Damascene (*On Heresies*) in the eighth, contended that, indeed, there were heretical groups that called themselves Christian yet practiced cannibalism and infant sacrifice.

The stories may have been urban legends, passed from time to time and place to place, keeping the plot while changing the players. One thing is certain: Such reports were sure to gain the attention of the pagan governors.

Most of the apologists responded to the hysteria with cool reason. Tertullian simply mocked its absurdity, inviting the credulous to join in the crazed rites of the Christians: "Come on! Plunge the knife into the baby, nobody's enemy, guilty of nothing, everybody's child . . . Catch the infant blood! Steep your bread with it! Eat and enjoy it!" (*Apology* 8.2).

The following passage from Lollianus is taken from Wilken (1984:18). Fronto's work is preserved in long quotations in the *Octavius* of Minucius Felix, a Church Father; the passage below is adapted from the 1892 Edinburgh edition of the Fathers. Celsus is from the reconstructed edition of *On the True Doctrine* by Hoffmann (1987:98).

Lollianus: Human Sacrifice

At this moment, another naked man arrived with a purple belt around his loins. He threw the boy's body on its back, struck it, opened it, removed the heart and placed it over the fire. Then he took the roasted heart off the fire and cut it into halves. He sprinkled it with barley and drenched it with oil. When it was sufficiently prepared, he distributed portions of it to the initiates; and when they were holding them (in their hands), he made them swear an oath by the blood of the heart. . . .

— FROM A PAPYRUS FRAGMENT

Fronto: Cannibals and Lechers

Surely this confederacy ought to be rooted out and denounced. They know one another by secret marks and insignia, and they love one another almost before they know one another. Everywhere they practice among themselves a lustful religion, and they call one another promiscuously "brothers and sisters." As they invoke that sacred name, even a more common debauchery becomes incestuous. Their foolish and senseless superstition revels in crime. I would not even speak of such things — which demand to be prefaced by an apology — unless truth were at the bottom of it.

I hear that they adore the head of an ass, that basest of creatures, consecrated by what silly persuasion, I do not know — a worthy and appropriate religion for such manners. Some say that they worship the male member of their pontiff and priest, and adore the nature, as it were, of their common parent. I know not whether these things are false, but certainly suspicion is applicable to secret and nocturnal rites. . . .

Now the story about the initiation of young novices is as much to be detested as it is well known. An infant is coated with flour, so as to deceive the unwary, and is placed before the person who is to be stained with their rites. This infant is slain by the young pupil urged on as if to harmless blows on the surface of the flour, which hides the wounds. Thirstily — O horror! — they lick up its blood. Eagerly, they divide its limbs. By this victim they are pledged together. With this consciousness of wickedness they are covenanted to mutual silence.

Such sacred rites as these are more foul than any sacrilege. And their banqueting is notorious as well, as all men speak of it everywhere. . . . On a solemn day, they assemble at the feast, with all their children, sisters, mothers, people of every sex and every age. There, after much feasting, when the fellowship has grown warm, and the fervor of incestuous lust has grown hot with drunkenness, they provoke a dog tied to the chandelier to jump and spring toward a small scrap of food thrown just beyond the reach of his chain. By this means the light is overturned and extinguished. In the shameless darkness, the connections of abominable lust involve them in the uncertainty of fate. Though not all commit incest, all are guilty of incest, since the desires of all provide the occasion for the actions of each.

— QUOTED IN MINUCIUS FELIX, *OCTAVIUS* 9

Celsus: Superstitious Wizardry

I have seen these Christian priests use books containing magical formulas and the names of various demons; they surely are up to no good and only mean to deceive good people by these tricks of theirs. I have this firsthand, from an Egyptian musician by the name of Dionysus. He testifies that magical ploys are especially effective among the illiterate and among those with shady moral characters. Those who have had anything to do with philosophy, on the other hand, are above such trickery.

— CELSUS

CHAPTER 18

St. Clement of Alexandria

A side from his abundant writings, we know little about Clement of Alexandria. Born around the year 150 into a pagan family, he received a broad and deep education in classical pagan culture. He converted to Christianity and placed himself under the tutelage of Pantaenus, the founder of the catechetical school in Alexandria, Egypt. Clement succeeded Pantaenus as rector of the school.

Clement's writings display his deep erudition. He quotes often from both the Old and New Testaments, as well as the pagan poets and philosophers. He shows an easy familiarity with the arts and sciences. He speaks frankly of everyday human realities, from marital intimacy to moneylending; and in his theology, he draws analogies from the worlds of culture, family, and business. In a passage below, he compares the Eucharist to mother's milk.

Clement wrote theology with an impassioned and poetic style. His extended metaphors are often stunning in their beauty. Like much poetry, however, they can also be enigmatic. Indeed, he admits in his work called the *Stromata* (meaning "Carpets") that he intentionally wrote in riddles. In order to respect the discipline of the secret, he would "here and there intersperse the dogmas . . . so that the discovery of the sacred traditions may not be easy to anyone of the uninitiated" (*Stromata* 7.18). This cryptic quality would remain with writers of the School of Alexandria for centuries, and would be raised to a fine art form by Clement's successor, Origen.

The hallmark of the Alexandrian school was its "allegorical" reading of the Old Testament, after the manner of Philo, a Jewish Platonist from first-century Alexandria. In reading the histories of Israel, Clement found many allegories, or "types," of the Eucharist. For example: "Melchizedek, king of Salem, priest of the Most High God, gave bread and wine, furnishing consecrated food for a type of the Eucharist" (*Stromata* 4.25; see Gen 14:18).

In some of his works, Clement so emphasizes the notion of spiritual sacrifices that he seems almost to exclude the possibility of ritual sacrifice such as the Mass. But his discussion of the Eucharist in most places renders such a reading highly improbable. His doctrine of the Eucharist was orthodox, if imprecise by modern standards. He lived in a time before circumstances — such as widespread heresy — pressed the Church to greater precision in doctrinal formulas.

Clement provides evidence that, even at an early date, the Church regulated the ritual of the liturgy. He condemns heretical rites as neither valid nor licit, because they contradict the rule, or canons, of the Church.

He was exiled during one of the Roman persecutions and died in Cappadocia before 215.

The following passages from his work are adapted from the 1892 Edinburgh edition of the Fathers.

Like Babies at the Breast

O mystic marvel! The universal Father is one, and one the universal Word; and the Holy Spirit is one and the same everywhere, and one is the only virgin mother. I love to call her the Church. This mother, when alone, had no milk, because alone she was not a woman. But she is once virgin and mother — pure as a virgin, loving as a mother. And calling her children to her, she nurses them with holy milk — with the Word for childhood.

Therefore, she had no milk; for the milk was this child fair and beautiful, the body of Christ, which nourishes by the Word the young brood, which the Lord himself brought forth in labor of the flesh, which the Lord himself swathed in his precious blood. O amazing birth! O holy swaddling bands!

The Word is all to the child, both father and mother and tutor and nurse. "Eat my flesh," he says, "and drink my blood" (Jn 6:32, 33, 36). Such is the suitable food that the Lord serves, and he offers his flesh and pours forth his blood, and nothing is wanting for the children's growth. O amazing mystery!

We are invited to cast off the old and bodily corruption, as well as the old food, receiving in exchange a new menu, that of Christ, receiving him if we can, to hide him within; so that, enshrining the Savior in our souls, we may correct the affections of our flesh.

You are not inclined to understand it this way, but perhaps more generally. Hear it also in another way. The flesh figuratively represents to us the Holy Spirit, for the flesh was created by him. The blood points out to us the Word, for as rich blood the Word has been infused into life; and the union of both is the Lord, the food of the infants — the Lord who is Spirit and Word. The food is the Lord Jesus — the Word of God, the Spirit made flesh, the heavenly flesh sanctified. This nourishment is the milk of the Father, by which alone we infants are fed.

The Word himself, then, the beloved One, and our nourisher, has shed his own blood for us, to save humanity. And we, believing in God, flee to the Word, "the care-soothing breast" of the Father. And he alone supplies us children with the milk of love, and those only are truly blessed who nurse at this breast. So Peter says: "So put away all malice and all guile and insincerity and envy and all slander. Like newborn babes, long for the pure spiritual milk, that by it you may grow up to salvation; for you have tasted that the Lord is Christ" (see 1 Pet 2:1-3).

— *THE TEACHER* 1.6

To Drink the Lord's Immortality

To drink the blood of Jesus is to partake in the Lord's immortality, for the Spirit is the vital principle of the Word, as blood is of flesh. Thus, as wine is blended with water, so is the Spirit with man. The one, the mixture of wine and water, nourishes to faith; while the other, the Spirit, conducts to immortality.

The mixture of both — the water and the Word — is called the Eucharist, the renowned and glorious grace. Those who receive it in faith are sanctified in body and soul.

— *THE TEACHER* 2.2

The False Eucharist of the Heretics

Now he who has fallen into heresy passes through an arid wilderness, abandoning the only true God. Destitute of God, he seeks waterless water, reaching an uninhabited and thirsty land, collecting sterility with his hands. And those destitute of prudence — those involved in heresies

— Wisdom urges, saying, "Stolen water is sweet, and bread eaten in secret is pleasant" (Prov 9:17). Thus, the Scripture clearly applies the terms bread and water to nothing else but to those heresies that employ bread and water in the oblation, violating the rule of the Church. For there are those who celebrate the Eucharist with mere water.

— *STROMATA* 1.19

Vote for Your Own Salvation

Imagine that your father comes up to you and says, "I sired you and raised you. Follow me, and join me in wickedness, and do not obey the law of Christ" — adding whatever a blasphemer, who is dead by nature, would say.

But on the other side hear the Savior: "I regenerated you, whom the world birthed badly for death. I freed, healed, and ransomed you. I will show you the face of the good Father God. Call no man your father on earth. Let the dead bury the dead. But follow me. For I will bring you to a rest of ineffable and unutterable blessings, which eye has not seen, nor ear heard, nor have entered into the human heart — which angels desire to look into, and see what good things God has prepared for the saints and the children who love him. I am he who feeds you, giving myself as bread, and he who tastes this bread experiences death no more. I am he who gives daily the drink of immortality. I am teacher of heavenly lessons. For you I contended with death, and paid your death, which you owed for your former sins and your unbelief towards God."

Having heard these considerations on both sides, decide for yourself and cast your vote for your own salvation.

—*WHO IS THE RICH MAN THAT SHALL BE SAVED* 23

CHAPTER 19

Origen of Alexandria

By even the most modest accounts, Origen was a prodigy. At eighteen, he was appointed rector of the most prestigious school in the Christian world, the school of catechumens in Alexandria, Egypt. Origen (185-254) was arguably the greatest biblical scholar of the Church's infant years. He compiled an edition of the Bible that included texts in six languages in parallel columns, and he produced thousands of books of Scripture commentary. He also taught philosophy, physics, rhetoric, mathematics, and astronomy. His biographers report that he kept six secretaries busy in his full-time employ.

Yet Origen was always controversial during his life, and he remains so even today.

He was the first Christian scholar to achieve celebrity status in the ancient world. Even the pagans respected him. The emperor's mother placed herself under his tutelage, as did the governor of Arabia.

Origen's fame surely aroused the envy of some fellow churchmen. Perhaps fame also emboldened him to pursue speculative theology to its outer reaches — and sometimes beyond.

His 6,000 books certainly gave him many occasions for misstep, especially in a time when speculative theology was just beginning to develop its language and methods. In later centuries, the Church would condemn certain propositions found in Origen: that creation was eternal; that the soul pre-existed the body; and that, at the end of time, all creation, even the devils, would be saved. His defenders, however, point to other passages in Origen's voluminous works that seem to contradict these propositions. Moreover, they point out that his intention was always to teach in accord with the Church, and to trust the Church more than his own tentative explorations. "We should accept as true only that which differs in no way from the tradition of the Church and the apostles" (*On First Things*, preface).

Origen is best known for his work in the spiritual interpretation of the Bible. The basic premise is that there are two "senses" to Scripture: the literal and the spiritual. While the literal sense tells of facts, events, and precepts, the deeper meaning — revealed by grace — tells of the mystical significance of the facts. In reading the Old Testament, Origen tended to emphasize Israel's people and history as allegories, foreshadowing realities that would be fully revealed only in Jesus Christ. Critics of Origen say he sometimes went too far in allegorizing the Old Testament, to the detriment of the literal sense of the text.

Origen did not invent the science of spiritual exegesis. Jesus himself gave spiritual interpretations of the Old Testament (see, for example, Jn 6:31-33, Lk 24:27). Other New Testament authors follow his lead (see 1 Cor 10:1-4; Heb 8:5; 1 Pet 3:20-21). Around the same time as the apostles, though independently, an Alexandrian Jew named Philo (d. 50) was methodically working through the books of the law to discern their allegorical and spiritual meaning.

In the details of the Old Testament, Origen often found signs foreshadowing the Eucharist — for example, in Israel's sojourn in the desert: "Then, in likeness, manna was food. Now, in reality, the flesh of the Word of God is true food.

As he himself says, 'my flesh is food indeed, and my blood is drink indeed'" (*On Numbers* 7.2). His homilies contain stunning passages uncovering the divine and eucharistic subtext of the sacrifices of ancient Israel.

Yet our appreciation of these works can be hampered by two things. One is Origen's trademark obscurity. Sometimes, his exegesis is so thick with his own peculiar, specialized vocabulary that it is impenetrable even to scholars. Consider this passage:

> The bread that the Divine Word declared to be identical with his body is the word nourishing souls, the word proceeding from the heavenly bread. . . . For the Divine Word did not declare his body to be the visible bread that he held in his hands, but the word in whose mystery that bread was to be broken (*On Matthew* 85).

Some critics of Origen (and some sympathetic heretics) have interpreted this passage as a denial of the Real Presence — though Origen elsewhere clearly affirms the Church's doctrine. The problem is that Origen's emphasis of the allegory does tend to overshadow the literal sense of the scriptural text, in this case, Matthew's account of the Last Supper.

The second problem is Origen's scrupulous observance of the discipline of the secret. In his homilies, he would usually stop just short of openly revealing the mysteries: "We conceal and pass over in silence the truths of deeper import when we see that our audience is composed of simpler minds" (*Against Celsus* 3:52). Thus, in the passages below, he begins the exegesis, but lets his listeners finish the process: "He who is inspired by the mysteries knows both the flesh and the blood of the Word of God. Therefore, let us not remain in these matters, which are known to the wise and cannot be laid open to the ignorant" (*On Leviticus* 10). "There is not much more to discuss about these things because it is enough to be understood by a single recollection" (ibid. 13).

After a series of disciplinary controversies, Origen was excommunicated by his own bishop. He found refuge in Palestine, where he was welcomed by the bishops there. He established a school in Caesarea that became, during his lifetime, the equal of the school in Alexandria. Origen died in 254 as a result of torture he suffered on account of the faith he had always loved.

His reputation has waxed and waned through the centuries. From age to age, he is alternately praised and condemned. The twentieth century saw something of an Origen revival, with the appreciative work of theologians such as Hans Urs von Balthasar, Henri de Lubac, and Jean Danielou. Origen has been cited increasingly often in recent papal documents, especially those of Pope John Paul II.

Passages from the *Homilies on Leviticus* are adapted from Barkley's translation (1990:198-9, 236-7) in The Catholic University of America Press *Fathers of the Church* series. The passage from the *Homilies on Exodus* is adapted from the translation used by Pierse (1909:66-67). All other passages are adapted from the excerpts in Pusey's *The Doctrine of the Real Presence as Contained in the Fathers* (1855).

A Mystical Interpretation

In the Israelite laws regarding sacrifice, Origen sees a foreshadowing of the Mass.

If the ancient custom of sacrifices is clear to you, let us see what these things also contain according to the mystical understanding. You heard that there were two sanctuaries: one visible and open to the priests; the other invisible and inaccessible. . . . I think this first sanctuary can be understood as this Church in which we are now placed in the flesh, in which the priests minister "at the altar of the whole burnt offerings" (see Ex 29:25), with that fire of which Jesus said, "I came to cast fire upon the earth, and how I wish that it were already kindled" (Lk 12:49). . . .

Do you want me to show you how the fire goes out from the words of the Holy Spirit and ignites the hearts of believers? Hear David speaking in the psalm: "The declaration of the Lord has set him on fire." And again in the Gospel it was written, after the Lord spoke to Cleopas, "Was not our heart burning within us when he opened the scriptures to us?" (Lk 24:18, 32). . . .

[But] whence is the fire kindled in you who never meditate on the divine declarations? On the contrary, what is more unfortunate is that you glow in the spectacles of the circus, in horse races, and in sports. And so this fire is not from the altar of the Lord, but it is that which is called an alien fire, and . . . those who brought "a foreign fire before the Lord were destroyed" (see Lev 16:1). You also burn when wrath fills you and when rage inflames you. Meanwhile you burn also with the love of the flesh, and you are cast away into the fires of most disgraceful passions. But all this is an alien fire and contrary to God. . . .

Therefore, the divine declaration says, "And he will place the incense upon the fire in the sight of the Lord, and the smoke of the incense will cover the mercy seat which is upon the [ark of the] covenant and he will not die. And he will take from the blood of the calf and will sprinkle it with his finger upon the mercy seat to the east" (Lev 16:13-14). Indeed, the ancients taught how the rite of atonement for men, which was done to God, should be celebrated.

But you who came to Christ, the true high priest, who made atonement for you to God by his blood and reconciled you to the Father, do not hold fast to the blood of the flesh. Learn rather the blood of the Word and hear him saying to you, "This is my blood which will be poured out for you for the forgiveness of sins" (Mt 26:28). He who is inspired by the mysteries knows both the flesh and the blood of the Word of God. Therefore, let us not remain in these matters, which are known to the wise and cannot be laid open to the ignorant.

— *ON LEVITICUS* 9-10

A Foreshadowing of Remembrance

The precept is given that, without ceasing, twelve loaves are placed in the sight of the Lord, so that the memory of the twelve tribes is always to be held before him. Through these things, a certain plea or supplication arises for each of the tribes. But an intercession of this kind is quite small and poor enough. For how much does it accomplish as a propitiation when the fruits of each tribe must be considered through a loaf and the works through the fruits?

But if these things are referred to the greatness of the mystery, you will find this "remembrance" to have the effect of a great propitiation. If you return to that bread "which comes down from heaven and gives life to the world" (Jn 6:33), that bread of the presence "whom God put forward as an expiation by his blood" (Rom

3:25), and if you turn your attention to that remembrance about which the Lord says, "Do this in remembrance of me" (1 Cor 11:25), you will find that this is the only "remembrance" that makes God gracious to men. Therefore, if you recall more intently the Church's mysteries, you will find the image of the future truth anticipated in these things written in the law. But there is not much more to discuss about these things because it is enough to be understood by a single recollection.

— *On Leviticus* 13

Hear the Word

You who are accustomed to attending the divine mysteries know how, when you receive the body of the Lord, you guard it with all care and reverence lest any small part should fall from it, lest any piece of the consecrated gift be lost. For you believe yourself guilty, and rightly so, if anything falls from there through your negligence. But if you are so careful to preserve his body, and rightly so, why do you think that there is less guilt to have neglected God's word than to have neglected his body?

— *On Exodus* 13.3

Always Keeping the Feast

Some object that we, too, have the custom of observing certain days — for example the Lord's day, the Preparation, the Passover, and Pentecost. To which I answer that the perfect Christian is always, in his thoughts, words, and deeds, serving his Lord, God the Word. All his days are the Lord's, and he is always keeping the Lord's day. He is unceasingly preparing himself for true life, and abstaining from the pleasures of this life, which lead astray so many. He does not indulge the lust of the flesh, but "pommeling his body and subduing it" (see 1 Cor 9:27). Thus he is always keeping the Preparation Day. Again, he who considers that "Christ, our paschal lamb, has been sacrificed" (1 Cor 5:7) knows that it is his duty to keep the feast by eating the flesh of the Word, and so he never ceases to keep the paschal feast. For *pascha* means passover, and he is ever striving in all his thoughts, words, and deeds, to pass over from the things of this life to God. He is hastening toward the city of God.

— *AGAINST CELSUS* 8.22

In the Upper Room

Jesus was about to celebrate with the disciples the feast whose symbol we enact, the Passover. After they asked, "Where do you want us to prepare for you the Passover?" he said, "Go, when a man carrying a jar of water meets you, follow him. He will show to you a large furnished room spread, cleaned, made ready. There prepare the Passover." Thus no one who enacts the Passover as Jesus wishes is in a room below. But if someone celebrates with Jesus, he is in a great room above, in a furnished room made clean, in a furnished room adorned and prepared. And if you go up with him in order to celebrate the Passover, he gives to you the cup of the New Covenant, he gives to you the bread of blessing, he makes a gift of his body and his blood. For this reason, let us urge you: Move up into the higher area, raise your eyes on high.

— *ON JEREMIAH* 19.13.4

Who Drinks Blood?

What people are accustomed to drinking blood? In the Gospel, the Jews who followed the Lord heard and were offended, and they said: "Who can eat flesh and drink blood?" But the Christian people, the faithful people, hear these things and embrace them, and follow him who says: "Unless you eat my flesh and drink my blood, you have no life in you; for my flesh is food indeed, and my blood is drink indeed" (see Jn 6:53, 55).

— *ON NUMBERS* 16.8

Evidence of the Kingdom

When you see gentiles coming into the faith, churches built, altars — not sprinkled with blood of cattle, but consecrated with the precious Blood of Christ — when you see priests and levites ministering, not with the blood of bulls and of goats, but the Word of God through the grace of the Holy Spirit, then say that Jesus succeeded Moses and obtained the princedom . . . Jesus the Son of God.

— *ON JOSHUA* 11.2

CHAPTER 20

St. Dionysius the Great

Dionysius was Origen's pupil and his successor as the rector of the Alexandrian school. He was named bishop of Alexandria in 247. During the persecutions, Dionysius was arrested and exiled twice. While fighting spiritual warfare against the Church's persecutors, he also faced the opposition of heretics as well as the ravages of an epidemic. He died in 265 and was hailed by later Fathers as a great teacher and pastor.

In the account below, adapted from the 1892 Edinburgh edition of the Fathers, he tells of how a man who had committed apostasy was, on his deathbed, received back to the sacraments.

To Fabius, Bishop of Antioch

I shall give an account of one particular case that occurred here. There was with us a certain Sarapion, an aged believer. He had spent his long life blamelessly, but had fallen in the time of trial [the persecution]. Often did this man pray [for absolution], and no one listened to him, for he had sacrificed to idols.

He fell sick and, for three successive days, lay mute and senseless. Recovering a little on the fourth day, he called his grandchild, and said, "My son, how long will you detain me? Hurry, I beg you, and absolve me quickly. Summon one of the priests for me." When he had said this, he became speechless again.

The boy ran for the priest; but it was night, and the man was sick, and was consequently unable to come. But I had issued an injunction, that persons at the point of death, if they requested absolution, and especially if they had earnestly sought it before, should be absolved, so that they might depart this life in cheerful hope. So the priest gave the boy a small portion of the Eucharist, telling him to steep it in water and drop it into the old man's mouth.

The boy returned bearing the portion. As he came near but before he had yet entered, Sarapion again recovered and said, "You have come, my child, and the priest was unable to come; but do quickly what you were instructed to do, and so let me depart." The boy steeped the morsel in water and immediately dropped it into the [old man's] mouth.

After he had swallowed a little of it, he gave up his spirit. Is it not obvious that he was preserved in life just until he could be absolved; and, with the sin wiped away, he could be acknowledged for the many good works he had done?

— *EPISTLE* 3

CHAPTER 21

Tertullian of Carthage

Tertullian (d. 222) stands in marked contrast to the Alexandrians. Where Clement and Origen were obscure and elusive, he is direct, literal, and blunt. The Alexandrians were poets and schoolmen; this Carthaginian was trained as a lawyer, and he loved a good argument.

Tertullian made a name for himself as a legal scholar in Rome. His prose was terse and always quotable. Some of his legal opinions found their way into the annals of the Roman court system. Converted from paganism around the year 193, he ever afterward made his case for Christianity.

The first of the great North African Christian writers, Tertullian wrote voluminously, defending the Church against its persecutors and arguing vigorously for unpopular and uncommon virtues, like virginity and patience. Yet he himself, as he readily admitted, lacked patience. Habitually contrarian and a rigorous moralist, he eventually argued his way out of communion with the Church, founding a sect, called the Tertullianists, within a schismatic movement called Montanism.

His arguments touched frequently, if briefly, upon matters related to the Eucharist, and so Tertullian left us a valuable record of the early liturgical practices in North Africa.

He made this clear: The priests said Mass daily, and Christians celebrated their liturgy at an altar. Only a priest could preside at the Mass. Mass was ordinarily offered before sunrise. The Mass included the sign of peace. The faithful were permitted to reserve the sacrament, to be consumed on the days when they did not attend Mass.

Tertullian had no qualms in revealing these incidentals, though he rarely went further in explicating the mysteries. He observed the discipline of the secret — "Silence is due to the sacred mysteries" (*Apology* 7) — but never in a coy way, and never drawing attention to his silence. He said as much as he could say, and he moved on. And, in a handful of places, he addressed scriptural passages that illumine the sacrament. In identifying the "daily bread" of the Lord's Prayer with the Eucharist, he passes along a commonplace of the early Church. This idea would, in time, be further developed by Tertullian's fellow North Africans, Cyprian (*On the Lord's Prayer* 18) and Augustine (*Harmony of the Gospels* 6.10).

Tertullian worried about the pastoral implications of eucharistic practices. He spoke to the scruples of those who fasted. He worried about what happened when people took the Eucharist home with them. He worried about how the sacred mysteries could remain secret within mixed marriages. Addressing wives with pagan husbands, he wrote: "Will not your husband know what you are secretly tasting before taking any food? And if he knows it to be bread, does he not believe it to be that bread which it is said to be?" (*To His Wife* 2.5).

Tertullian spoke of the Real Presence in graphically realistic terms: "The flesh feeds on the body of Christ so that the soul might grow fat on God" (*On the Resurrection of the Body* 8). In some places, however, he wrote with an imprecision that would be unacceptable in a later age, calling the eucharistic species a "figure" or "image" of Christ's Body. But, in the early third century, theology lacked a technical vocabulary for discussing the sacramental reality of the Eucharist. So even Tertullian — a man who coined many technical theological terms (most notably, Trinity) — sometimes fell short of a mark that was set in later centuries.

Believing that he had found the true "Church of the Spirit," Tertullian apparently never reconciled with what he called the "Church of a bunch of bishops." He died excommunicated some time after 220.

The following excerpts are adapted from the 1892 Edinburgh edition of the Fathers.

The Lord's Prayer

How gracefully has the divine Wisdom arranged the order of the prayer; so that after things heavenly — that is, after the name of God, the will of God, and the kingdom of God — it should give earthly necessities also room for a petition.

For the Lord had issued his edict, "Seek his kingdom, and these things shall be yours as well" (Lk 12:31), so that, spiritually, we may rather understand, "Give us this day our daily bread."

Christ is our Bread; because Christ is Life, and bread is life. "I am," he said, "the bread of life" (Jn 6:35). And a little bit before, "The bread of God is that which comes down from heaven, and gives life to the world" (Jn 6:33). Then we find, too, that his body is reckoned as bread: "This is my body" (Mt 26:26).

So, in petitioning for "daily bread," we ask for perpetuity in Christ, inseparable from his body. But, because that word admits a bodily sense, too, it cannot be so used without the religious remembrance of spiritual discipline; for the Lord commands that we pray for the bread that is the only food necessary for believers. "For the Gentiles seek all these things" (Mt 6:32).

— *ON PRAYER* 6

In the Early Morning

We assemble before daybreak, and take the sacrament of the Eucharist from the hand of none but those who preside. This the Lord commanded to be eaten at meal-times and urged to be taken by everyone.

— *THE CHAPLET* 3

The Eucharist Does Not Break a Fast

Most of those who fast think that they must not be present at the sacrificial prayers, because their fast would be dissolved by reception of the Lord's body. But does the Eucharist cancel a service devoted to God, or bind it more to God? Will not your fast be more solemn if you have stood at God's altar when the Lord's body has been received and reserved? Each point, then, is secured, both participation in the sacrifice and the discharge of duty.

— *ON PRAYER* 19

The Sign of Peace

It has become a prevalent custom for those who are fasting to withhold the kiss of peace — which is the seal of the prayer they have made with the brethren. But . . . what prayer is complete if divorced from the "holy kiss" (1 Cor 16:20)? Whom does peace keep from rendering service to his Lord? From what kind of sacrifice do men depart without peace? However good our prayer may be, it will not be better than the observance of the precept that bids us to conceal our fasts. When we abstain from the kiss, people know we are fasting.

— *On Prayer* 18

Body and Blood Prefigured

Here, Tertullian defends the Old Testament witness to the Eucharist against the attacks of Marcionism, one of the very early heresies. Marcion (d. 160) taught that the God of Israel was evil, the religion of Israel demonic, and the Old Testament useless. His errors lived on in heretical sects for centuries after his death.

When [Jesus] earnestly expressed his desire to eat the Passover, he considered it his own feast; for it would have been unworthy of God to want what was not his own. Then, taking the bread and giving it to his disciples, he made it his own body, by saying, "This is my body" — that is, the figure of my body. There could not have been a figure, however, unless there had first been a true body. An empty thing or a phantom is incapable of a figure.

If, however, (as Marcion might say) he pretended the bread was his body, because he lacked any true bodily substance, it follows that he must have given bread for us. It would contribute very well to the support of Marcion's theory of a phantom body, that bread should have been crucified! But why call his body bread and not a melon, which Marcion must have had instead of a heart?

Marcion did not understand how ancient was this figure of the body of Christ, who said himself through Jeremiah: "I was like a gentle lamb led to the slaughter.

I did not know it was against me they devised schemes, saying, Let us cast the tree upon his bread" (see Jer 11:19), which means, of course, the cross upon his body. Thus, casting light, as always, upon the ancient prophecies, he declared plainly what he meant by the bread, when he called the bread his own body.

Likewise, when mentioning the cup and making the new covenant to be sealed in his blood, he affirms the reality of his body. For no blood can belong to a body that is not a body of flesh. A body without flesh would not possess blood. Thus, from the evidence of the flesh, we get a proof of the body, and a proof of the flesh from the evidence of the blood.

In order, however, that you may discover how, in ancient days, wine was used to symbolize blood, turn to Isaiah, who asks, "Who is this that comes from Edom, in crimsoned garments from Bozrah, he that is glorious in his apparel, marching in the greatness of his strength? . . . Why is your apparel red, and your garments like his that treads in the wine press?" (Is 63:1-2). The prophetic Spirit contemplates the Lord as if he were already on his way to his passion, clad in his bodily nature; and since that is how he would suffer, he represents the bleeding condition of his flesh —under the metaphor of garments dyed red — as if reddened in the treading and crushing of the wine press, from which laborers descend reddened with juice, like bloodstained men.

More clearly still does the Book of Genesis foretell this, when it delineated Christ in the person of the patriarch [Judah], saying, "He washes his garments in wine, and his vesture in the blood of grapes" (Gen 49:11). In his garments and clothes, the prophecy pointed out his flesh; in the wine, his blood. Thus, he now consecrates his blood in wine, who then used the figure of wine to describe his blood.

— *AGAINST MARCION* 4.40

The Flesh Feeds on Christ's Body

Once more, against the heretics who disdained the human body, Tertullian gloried in the flesh of Christ, crucified and risen — and given in the Eucharist.

A soul cannot gain salvation unless it believes while it is in the flesh. Flesh is the very condition on which salvation hinges. And since the soul is, as a consequence of its salvation, chosen for the service of God, it is the flesh that actually makes it capable of such service. The flesh is washed so that the soul may be cleansed. The flesh is anointed so that the soul may be consecrated. The flesh is signed (with the cross) so that the soul too may be fortified; the flesh is overshadowed with the laying-on of hands so that the soul may be enlightened by the Spirit. The flesh feeds on the body of Christ so that the soul might grow fat on God.

— *ON THE RESURRECTION OF THE FLESH* 8.2

Scandalous Communion

Zeal for the faith moves us to . . . mourn that a Christian should come from idols into the Church; should come from an adversary workshop into the house of God; should raise to God the Father hands that are the mothers of idols; should pray to God with hands that, outside, are prayed to in opposition to God; should apply to the Lord's body hands that confer bodies on demons!

Nor is this sufficient. Let's say that it be a small matter, if they contaminate what they receive from other hands; but those very hands even deliver to others what they have contaminated. Idol-makers are chosen even for the Church's orders. O wickedness! Once did the Jews lay hands on Christ; but these mangle his body daily. O hands to be cut off! Hear the saying, "If your right hand causes you to sin, cut it off" (Mt 5:30). . . . What hands need more to be amputated than those that visit scandal upon the Lord's body?

— *ON IDOLATRY* 7

CHAPTER 22

St. Cyprian of Carthage

A third-century bishop of Carthage, Cyprian considered himself a student of Tertullian. When he wanted to read the old lawyer's works, he would say, "Bring the Master to me." Cyprian's work everywhere shows the influence of Tertullian. He follows his master, for example, in his eucharistic interpretation of the Lord's Prayer.

Unlike Tertullian, however, Cyprian believed the visible unity of the Church to be of paramount importance. The Church received that unity, according to Cyprian, from the sacrament of the Eucharist. Moreover, Cyprian accepted with utmost gravity the very office of bishop that Tertullian had held in contempt.

Cyprian served as bishop from 248 to 258, ten years of intermittently intense persecutions and devastating plague in North Africa. Because of these challenges, he urged the people of his diocese to frequent Communion, which would be their strength in moments of trial.

Some, after all, were failing the test of faith and committing acts of idolatry in order to save their lives. These people were commonly called the *lapsi*, "the fallen," and many sought afterward to be readmitted to the sacraments.

Meanwhile, Cyprian's Church included others who had survived torture without abandoning the faith. These, called "confessors," were esteemed by their fellow Christians and sometimes accorded great authority because of the witness they had given.

Some of the confessors opposed the readmission of *lapsi* until they were in imminent danger of death. The *lapsi* had sinned grievously, the confessors argued, and so must pass the rest of their lives in public penance. To give them the Eucharist would cause a scandal.

Popular sympathy was divided, and the controversy raged in the region of Carthage. Cyprian finally ruled that the *lapsi* should be welcomed back after a period of penance that was significantly shorter than lifelong. The duration would depend upon the circumstances of an individual's apostasy. The bishop chose this course because he believed that the *lapsi* needed the sacrament — so that, if called again to choose between Christ and Caesar, they would then choose Christ.

Of course, only a valid Eucharist could provide strength. Thus, Cyprian was much concerned with the rapid spread of heresies that attempted to mimic the sacraments. Several sects, for example, were offering the sacrifice with water alone, rather than wine mixed with water. In a long letter to a priest of his diocese, Cyprian condemns water-only liturgies on several grounds: They contradict the prophecies of the Old Testament, the model of the New Testament, and the witness of tradition. Moreover, the heretics confused what Christ had intended the sacraments to signify; for water fails to suggest blood, but overwhelmingly does suggest the washing and the birth of baptism. Cyprian demonstrates that any tinkering with the symbolism of the sacraments will have devastating consequences — in theology and in life.

Cyprian's works provide a summary of the biblical interpretation at the foundation of the early Church's eucharistic doctrine and worship. Yet his great contribution is in thinking through the pastoral applications of the Church's teaching on the sacrament.

Cyprian died a martyr in 258. The following excerpts are adapted from the 1892 Edinburgh edition of the Fathers.

Our Father . . .

As the [Lord's Prayer] proceeds, we ask, "Give us this day our daily bread." This may be understood both spiritually and literally, because either way of understanding it is rich in divine usefulness to our salvation. For Christ is the bread of life; and this bread does not belong to all men, but it is ours. And just as we say "Our Father," since he is the Father of those who understand and believe, so also we call it "our bread," since Christ is the bread of those who are in union with his body.

We ask that this bread should be given to us daily, that we who are in Christ and daily receive the Eucharist for the food of salvation may not be kept, by the obstacle of some heinous sin, from communion with the heavenly bread, and thus be separated from Christ's body. For he himself predicts and warns, "I am the living bread which came down from heaven; if any one eats of this bread, he will live for ever; and the bread which I shall give for the life of the world is my flesh" (Jn 6:51).

When he says that whoever eats of his bread shall live forever, he makes clear that those who partake of his body and receive the Eucharist, by the right of that Communion, are living. On the other hand, we must fear and pray for anyone withheld from Communion and separated from Christ's body, lest they should remain at a distance from salvation. He himself threatens: "Unless you eat the flesh of the Son of man and drink his blood, you have no life in you" (Jn. 6:53). So we ask that our bread — that is, Christ — may be given to us daily, that we who abide and live in Christ may not depart from his sanctification and body.

— ON THE LORD'S PRAYER 18

Strength in Warfare

Cyprian urges a priest not to deny the Eucharist to those in dire need — the repentant who are at risk of arrest by the civil authorities.

The sheep must not be deserted by the shepherds in times of danger. Rather, the whole flock must be gathered together into one place, that the Lord's army may arrive for the contest of heavenly warfare. The repentance of mourners was reasonably prolonged for a more extensive time. Help was given to the sick only at the point of their departure. Peace and tranquility prevailed, then, permitting the long postponement of the tears of the mourners, and late assistance in sickness to the dying.

But now peace is necessary, not only for the sick, but for the strong. Nor is Communion to be granted by us only to the dying, but to the living. We must not stir them up and urge them to battle, only to leave them unarmed and naked. Rather, let us fortify them with the protection of Christ's body and blood. This is the very purpose of the Eucharist — that it may be a safeguard to those who receive it. So we must arm, with the protection of the Lord's abundance, those whom we wish to be safe against the enemy. For how do we teach or provoke them to shed their blood in confession of his name, if we deny the blood of Christ to those who are about to enter warfare? Or how do we make them fit for the cup of martyrdom, if we do not first let them drink, in the Church, the cup of the Lord by the right of Communion?

We should make a distinction, dearest brother. On the one hand, we have those who have committed apostasy and returned to living heathen lives in the world which they had renounced, and others who are deserters to the heretics, daily taking up parricidal arms against the Church. Yet, on the other hand, there are those who do not depart from the Church's threshold, and constantly and sorrowfully beg divine and paternal consolation, professing that they are now prepared for the battle and ready to stand and fight bravely for the name of their Lord and for their own salvation.

In these times we grant peace, not to those who sleep, but to those who watch. We grant peace, not amid indulgences, but amid arms. We grant peace, not for rest, but for the field of battle. If, according to what we hear, and desire, and believe of them, they shall stand bravely, and shall overthrow the adversary alongside us, we shall not repent of having granted peace to men so brave.

It is the great honor and glory of our episcopate to have granted peace to martyrs, so that we, as priests who daily celebrate the sacrifices of God, may prepare offerings and victims for God. But may the Lord forbid that any of the brethren who have lapsed should seek peace through deception — that they, in a time of impending struggle, should receive peace without any intention of doing battle. Such a man betrays and deceives himself, hiding one thing in his heart and pronouncing another with his voice.

We, for our part, can only judge by looking upon the face of each one. We cannot scrutinize the heart and inspect the mind. Concerning these, the Discerner and Searcher of hidden things judges, and he will quickly come and judge the secret, hidden things of the heart. Evil should not stand in the way of good, but rather evil should be overcome by good. Peace, therefore, should not be denied to those who are about to endure martyrdom.

— Letter 53.2-5, *to Cornelius*

A Call to Martyrdom

Let us take these arms, let us fortify ourselves with these spiritual and heavenly safeguards, that in the most evil day we may be able to withstand and resist the threats of the devil. Let us put on the breastplate of righteousness, that our breast may be fortified and safe against the darts of the enemy. Let our feet be shod with Gospel teaching, and armed, so that, when we shall begin to trample and crush the serpent, he may not be able to bite and trip us up. Let us bravely bear the shield of faith, whose protection extinguishes anything the enemy darts at us. Let us protect our head with the helmet of salvation, that our ears may be guarded from hearing the deadly edicts; that our eyes may be fortified, that they may not see the odious images; that our brow may be fortified, so as to keep safe the sign of God; that our mouth may be fortified, that the conquering tongue may confess Christ as Lord. Let us arm the right hand with the sword of the Spirit, that it may bravely reject the deadly sacrifices; that, mindful of the Eucharist, the hand that has received the Lord's body may embrace the Lord himself, hereafter to receive from the Lord the reward of heavenly crowns.

— Letter 55.9, *to the people of Thibaris*

On the Chalice of the Lord

This tract, addressed to the priest Cecilius, is the only document of the first two Christian centuries that deals exclusively with the celebration of the Mass (Quasten 1952:II, 381).

Cyprian to Cecilius his brother, greeting!

The bishops have been placed by divine condescension over the Lord's churches throughout the world, and I know, dearest brother, that very many of them keep to the plan of Gospel truth and the tradition of the Lord. They do not introduce human novelties or depart from what Christ our Master prescribed and did.

Yet some do not do as Jesus Christ, our Lord and God, the author and teacher of this sacrifice, did and taught. They do so through ignorance or simplicity in consecrating the chalice of the Lord and ministering to the people. Thus, I find it a religious duty to write you this letter, so that, if anyone remains in this error, he may see the light of truth, and return to the root and origin of the tradition of the Lord.

You must not think, dearest brother, that I am writing thoughts that are merely mine or merely human, or that I am boldly taking this on of my own will. I always hold my mediocrity with lowly and modest moderation. But when anything is prescribed by the inspiration and command of God, a faithful servant must obey the Lord, acquitted by all of assuming anything arrogantly to himself. For he should fear offending the Lord unless he does as commanded.

Know, then, that I have been admonished that, in offering the cup, the tradition of the Lord must be observed, and that we must do nothing but what the

Lord first did on our behalf. Thus, the cup that we offer in remembrance of him should be offered mingled with wine. Christ says, "I am the true vine" (Jn 15:1), so the blood of Christ is assuredly not water, but wine. Neither can his blood — by which we are redeemed and given life — appear to be in the cup when the cup holds no wine. The wine shows forth the blood of Christ, which is declared by the sacrament and testimony of all the Scriptures.

The Old Testament Prophecy

We find in Genesis, in the story of Noah, a precursor and figure of the Lord's passion in regard to the sacrament. We see that he drank wine; he was drunk; he was stripped naked in his household; he was lying down with his thighs naked and exposed; the nakedness of the father was observed by his second son and was told abroad, but was covered by two other sons, the eldest and the youngest; and other matters which it is not necessary to trace out. It is enough for us to embrace only that Noah, setting forth a type of the future truth, did not drink water, but wine, and thus expressed the figure of the passion of the Lord.

In the priest Melchizedek, too, we see prefigured the sacrament of the sacrifice of the Lord. Divine Scripture testifies: "And Melchizedek king of Salem brought out bread and wine" (Gen 14:18). A priest of the Most High God, he blessed Abraham. And the Holy Spirit declares in the Psalms that Melchizedek bore a type of Christ, saying from the person of the Father to the Son: "Before the morning star I begot you. . . . You are a priest for ever after the order of Melchizedek" (Ps 109:3-4). This order, indeed, comes from that sacrifice, thence descending because Melchizedek was a priest of the Most High God; because he offered wine and bread; and because he blessed Abraham. For who is more a priest of the Most High God than our Lord Jesus Christ? He offered a sacrifice to God the Father, and offered that very same thing that Melchizedek had offered: bread and wine — that is, his body and blood. . . . Completing and fulfilling this action, the Lord offered bread and the cup mixed with wine. He who is the fullness of truth fulfilled the truth of the image prefigured.

Moreover, through Solomon, the Holy Spirit shows forth the type of the Lord's sacrifice, making mention of the immolated victim, the bread and wine, and even the altar and the apostles, saying, "Wisdom has built her house, she has set up her seven pillars. She has slaughtered her beasts, she has mixed her wine, she has also set her table. She has sent out her maids to call from the highest places in the town, 'Whoever is simple, let him turn in here!' To him who is without sense she says, 'Come, eat of my bread and drink of the wine I have mixed' " (Prov 9:1-5). In declaring the wine mingled, he prophetically foretells the cup of the Lord mingled with water and wine, that it may appear that our Lord's passion had accomplished what had been predicted beforehand.

This same thing is signified in the blessing of Judah, which expresses another figure of Christ: that he should have praise and worship from his brethren; that he should press down the back of his enemies yielding and fleeing, with the hands with which he bore the cross and conquered death; and that he himself is the Lion of the tribe of Judah, and should rest sleeping in his passion; that he should rise up, and should himself be the hope of the Gentiles. To these, the divine Scripture adds, "He washes his garments in wine and his vesture in the blood of grapes" (Gen 49:11). But when the blood of the grape is mentioned, what else could that mean but the wine of the chalice of the blood of the Lord?

In Isaiah also, the Holy Spirit testifies this same thing concerning the Lord's passion, saying, "Why is your apparel red, and your garments like his that treads in the wine press?" (Is 63:2). Can water make garments red? Or is it water in the wine press to be pressed out or trampled underfoot? Surely, wine is mentioned so that the Lord's blood may be understood, and so that the prophets might understand and foretell what would afterward be shown in the chalice of the Lord. The treading and pressure of the wine press arise repeatedly because wine cannot be prepared unless the bunch of grapes are first trampled and pressed. Neither could we drink the blood of Christ unless Christ had first been trampled and pressed, and had first drunk the cup of which he should also give believers to drink.

But whenever the holy Scripture names water, it refers to baptism, as we see intimated in Isaiah: "Remember not," he says, "the former things, nor consider the things of old. Behold, I am doing a new thing; now it springs forth, do you not perceive it? I will make a way in the wilderness and rivers in the desert. The wild beasts will honor me, the jackals and the ostriches; for I give water in the wilderness, rivers in the desert, to give drink to my chosen people, the people whom I formed for myself that they might declare my praise" (Is 43:18-21). There God foretold, through the prophet, that among the nations, in places which previously had been dry, rivers should afterward flow plenteously, and

should provide water for the elected people of God —
that is, for those who were made sons of God by the
generation of baptism.

It is again predicted and foretold that the Jews, if
they should thirst and seek after Christ, should drink
with us and attain the grace of baptism. "If they shall
thirst," he says, "he shall lead them through the deserts,
shall bring forth water for them out of the rock; the rock
shall be cloven, and the water shall flow, and my people
shall drink" (see Is 48:21). This is fulfilled in the Gospel,
when Christ, who is the Rock, is cloven by a stroke of
the spear in His passion. . . .

The New Testament Model

But there is no need for many arguments, dearest
brother, to prove that baptism is always indicated by the
naming of water, and that that is how we should understand it. The Lord, when he came, manifested the truth
of baptism and the cup in commanding that that faithful
water, the water of eternal life, should be given to believers in baptism; but he taught by the example of his own
authority that the cup should be mingled with a union of
wine and water. Taking the cup on the eve of his passion,
he blessed it, and gave it to his disciples, saying, "Drink of
it, all of you; for this is my blood of the covenant, which
is poured out for many for the forgiveness of sins. I tell
you I shall not drink again of this fruit of the vine until
that day when I drink it new with you in my Father's
kingdom" (Mt 26:27-29). We find that the cup which
the Lord offered was mixed, and that it was wine that he
called his blood. So it seems that the blood of Christ is
not offered if there is no wine in the cup, nor the Lord's
sacrifice celebrated with a legitimate consecration unless

our oblation and sacrifice correspond to his passion. How, after all, shall we drink the new wine of the fruit of the vine with Christ in the kingdom of his Father if we do not offer wine in the sacrifice of God the Father and of Christ, nor mix the cup of the Lord according to the Lord's own tradition?

The blessed apostle Paul, chosen and sent by the Lord and appointed a preacher of the Gospel truth, lays down these very things in his epistle, saying, "The Lord Jesus on the night when he was betrayed took bread, and when he had given thanks, he broke it, and said, 'This is my body which is for you. Do this in remembrance of me.' In the same way also the cup, after supper, saying, 'This cup is the new covenant in my blood. Do this, as often as you drink it, in remembrance of me.' For as often as you eat this bread and drink the cup, you proclaim the Lord's death until he comes" (1 Cor 11:23-26). It is commanded, then, by the Lord, and confirmed and delivered by his apostle, that as often as we drink, we do, in remembrance of the Lord, the same thing the Lord did. Thus, we do not accomplish what the Lord commanded unless we do what the Lord did, mixing his cup in the same way and never departing from the divine teaching. We must never stray from the Gospel precepts. Disciples ought to observe and do the same things the Master both taught and did. The blessed apostle, in another place, more earnestly and strongly teaches, saying, "I am astonished that you are so quickly deserting him who called you in the grace of Christ and turning to a different gospel — not that there is another gospel, but there are some who trouble you and want to pervert the gospel of Christ. But even if we, or an angel from heaven, should preach to you a gospel contrary to that which we preached to you, let him be accursed. As we have said before, so now I say again, If any one is preaching to you a gospel contrary to that which you received, let him be accursed" (Gal 1:6-9).

The Contemporary Situation

Neither the apostle himself nor an angel from heaven can preach or teach otherwise than Christ has once taught and his apostles have announced. So I wonder very much where this practice started, which, contrary to Gospel and apostolic discipline, water is offered in some places in the Lord's cup. For water by itself cannot express the blood of Christ. . . .

How perverse and contrary it is, that although the Lord at the marriage made wine of water (see Jn 2), we should make water of wine, when even the sacrament of that thing ought to admonish and instruct us rather to offer wine in the sacrifices of the Lord. . . . For because Christ bore us all, in bearing our sins, we see that the water represents the people, while the wine manifests the blood of Christ. When the water is mingled in the cup with wine, the people are made one with Christ, and the assembly of believers is associated and joined with him in whom it believes. This association and joining of water and wine is so mingled in the Lord's cup that that mixture cannot any more be separated. Similarly, nothing can separate the Church — that is, the people established in the Church, faithfully and firmly persevering in that which they have believed — from Christ, in such a way as to prevent their undivided love from always abiding and adhering.

Thus, therefore, in consecrating the cup of the Lord, water alone cannot be offered, even as wine alone cannot be offered. For if anyone offer wine only, the blood of Christ is dissociated from us; but if the water is alone, the people are dissociated from Christ. When both are mingled, and joined with one another by a close union, there is completed a spiritual and heavenly sacrament. Thus, the cup of the Lord is not indeed water alone, nor wine alone, but each mingled with the other. On the other hand, the body of the Lord cannot be flour alone or water alone, unless both should be united and joined together and compacted in the mass of one bread; for in this very sacrament our people are shown to be unified. As many grains are collected, ground, and mixed together into one mass to make one bread, so in Christ, who is the heavenly bread, we may know that there is one body, with which our number is joined and united.

There is, then, no reason, dearest brother, for anyone to follow the custom of those who have thought that water alone should be offered in the cup of the Lord. For we must inquire whom they themselves have followed. For in the sacrifice that Christ offered none is to be followed but Christ. . . .

The discipline of all religion and truth is overturned unless what is spiritually prescribed is faithfully observed; unless indeed anyone should fear in the morning sacrifices, lest by the taste of wine he should be redolent of the blood of Christ. Thus, the brotherhood is even beginning to hold back from the passion of Christ in persecutions, by learning in the offerings to be disturbed concerning his blood and his blood-shedding. Moreover, however, the Lord says in the Gospel, "Whoever is ashamed of me . . . of him will the Son of man also be ashamed" (Mk 8:38). And the apostle also speaks, saying, "If I were still pleasing men, I should not be a servant of Christ" (Gal

1:10). But how can we shed our blood for Christ, who blush to drink the blood of Christ? . . .

Because we make mention of his passion in all sacrifices (for the Lord's passion is the sacrifice we offer), we ought to do nothing else than what he did. For Scripture says, "For as often as you eat this bread and drink the cup, you proclaim the Lord's death until he comes" (1 Cor 11:26). As often, therefore, as we offer the cup in commemoration of the Lord and of his passion, let us do what we know the Lord did.

— *Letter to Cecilius*

Unworthy Communion

Listen to something that happened when I myself was present and a witness. Some parents who were fleeing [persecution] — and were careless on account of their terror — left a little daughter under the care of a wet-nurse. The nurse turned the forsaken child over to the magistrates. Then, in the shrine of an idol, where the crowds were flocking to damn themselves, they fed the child bread soaked in wine, since she was too young to eat meat. Afterward, the mother recovered her child. But the girl was unable to speak or even to indicate the crime that had been committed, a crime she had been unable to understand or to prevent. So it happened unawares in their ignorance, that when we were offering the sacrifice, the mother brought it in with her. Meanwhile, the girl mingled with the saints and became impatient with our prayer and supplications. At one moment she shook with weeping, and at another she tossed about like a wave of the sea by the violent excitement of her mind. It was as if a torturer compelled the soul of that tender child to con-

179

fess her consciousness of the fact with whatever signs she could. When the solemnities were finished, the deacon began to offer the cup to those present. When her turn came, the little child, by the prompting of the divine majesty, turned away her face and refused the cup, pressing her mouth closed with resisting lips. Still the deacon persisted and, against her will, forced on her some of the sacrament of the cup. Then there followed a sobbing and vomiting. In a profane body and mouth the Eucharist could not remain. The drink sanctified as the blood of the Lord burst forth from the polluted stomach. So great is the Lord's power, so great is his majesty! The secrets of darkness were disclosed under his light, and not even hidden crimes deceived God's priest.

This is true of an infant, who was not yet old enough to speak of the crime committed against her by others. But the woman who, late in life and advanced in age, secretly crept in among us when we were offering the sacrifice, received not food, but a sword for herself. It was as if she had taken some deadly poison into her jaws and body and began presently to be tortured, stiffened with frenzy. No longer suffering the misery of persecution, she shivered and trembled from her crime and fell down. The crime of her lying conscience was not long unpunished or concealed. She who had deceived man felt that God was taking vengeance.

Another woman tried with unworthy hands to open the box in which she kept the holy (body) of the Lord, and was deterred from touching it by fire rising up from it. And when another, who himself was defiled, dared with the rest to receive secretly a part of the sacrifice celebrated by the priest, he could not eat nor handle the holy of the Lord. He opened his hands to find a cinder.

This experience shows that the Lord withdraws when he is denied; nor does the undeserving receive any benefit for salvation, since saving grace is changed by the departure of holiness into a cinder.

How many people every day do not repent or confess their crimes and are filled with unclean spirits? How many are shaken even to insanity and idiocy by the raging of madness? Nor is there any need to go through the deaths of individuals. The punishment of their sins is as varied as the multitude of sinners is abundant. Let each one consider not what another has suffered, but what he himself deserves to suffer. Nor should anyone think that he has escaped if his punishment is delayed for a time. Indeed he should fear it even more, since the wrath of God the judge has reserved it for himself.

— *On the Lapsed* 25-26

Shun Those in Schism

The Lord's sacrifices themselves declare that Christians are of one mind, linked together by a firm and inseparable charity. For when the Lord calls bread his own body — bread that is gathered from many grains — he signifies that our people, whom he bore, are united. When he calls the wine his blood — wine that is pressed from many grapes and clusters and collected together — he also signifies our flock linked together by the mingling of a united multitude . . . . Truly, how inseparable is the sacrament of unity, and how hopeless are those who cause a schism and forsake their bishop, appointing another in his place. What extreme ruin they earn for themselves from the indignation of God. Holy Scripture declares in the books of Kings that ten tribes were divided from the tribe of Judah and Benjamin. They abandoned their king and appointed for themselves another one. "And the Lord rejected all the descendants of Israel, and afflicted them, and gave them into the hand of spoilers, until he had cast them out of his sight. When he had torn Israel from the house of David they made Jerobo'am the son of Nebat king" (2 Kings 17:20-21). It says that the Lord was very angry, and gave them up to perdition, because they were scattered from unity, and had made another king for themselves. So great was the Lord's indignation against those who had made the schism, that even when the man of God was sent to Jerobo'am, to accuse him of his sins and predict the future vengeance, he was forbidden to eat bread or to drink water with them. And when he did not observe this and took meat in violation of God's command, he was immediately struck down by the majesty of the divine judgment. On his return, he was slain by the jaws of a lion that attacked him. Does anyone dare to say that the saving water of baptism and heavenly grace can be shared with schismatics — with whom neither earthly food nor worldly drink ought to be in common?

— *Letter to Magnus* 6

CHAPTER 23

St. Cornelius of Rome

Cornelius was elected pope in 251, after the see of Rome had been vacant for more than a year. It was a time of intense persecution, and the Church was divided over how to deal with Christians who had denied the faith under torture or threat of death. Cornelius favored receiving them back to Communion after a long period of penance. Many Christians opposed him, however, insisting that Christians guilty of mortal sin should not be forgiven during the course of their earthly lives. An intellectual leader of the opposition, the Roman priest Novatian, persuaded a small group of clergy to proclaim him as their pope. Cornelius wrote to the bishops of the major sees in the world — including Cyprian in Carthage and Dionysius in Alexandria — in order to gain their support and inform them of Novatian's tactics. His letter to Fabius of Antioch, preserved in the *Church History* of Eusebius, includes the chilling image of Novatian insisting that his adherents swear an oath on the Eucharist that they would never return to Cornelius.

The excerpt below is based on the translation of Eusebius in the 1892 Edinburgh edition of the Fathers.

A Blasphemous Oath

This illustrious man [Novatian] abandoned God's Church, in which, when he believed, he was judged worthy of the priesthood through the favor of the bishop who ordained him to the priestly office. This had been resisted by all the clergy and many of the laity, because it was unlawful that one who had been confined to a sickbed should enter into the order of the clergy. But the bishop requested permission to ordain this one only . . .

When he has made the offerings and distributed a portion to each person, he compels the unfortunates to swear an oath in place of the blessing. Holding their hands in his own, he will not release them until they have sworn this way (I give you his own words): "Swear to me by the body and blood of our Lord Jesus Christ that you will never forsake me and turn to Cornelius." And the unfortunate man does not taste until he has called down curses on himself; and instead of saying "Amen" as he takes the bread, he says, "I will never return to Cornelius." . . .

But know that he has now been made bare and desolate. The brethren leave him every day and return to the Church. The blessed martyr named Moses, who lately suffered among us a glorious and admirable martyrdom, while he was still alive, saw through his boldness and folly, and refused to commune with him and the five priests who had joined him in separating themselves from the Church.

— Eusebius, *Church History* 6.43

CHAPTER 24

St. Firmilian of Caesarea

Firmilian was a contemporary and a correspondent of Cyprian. As bishop of Caesarea in Cappadocia (in modern Turkey), he held an influential position in the Church. He was a friend from youth of Gregory of Pontus. Both men became students and disciples of Origen. As bishop, Firmilian brought Origen to his see for a stint of teaching; and later Firmilian himself took leave to study further with Origen in Palestine. Firmilian played an active role in many doctrinal and disciplinary disputes that arose in his day. He opposed Novatian, the rigorist Roman priest and pretender to the papacy. Still, he was briefly excommunicated for favoring the rebaptism of those who had been baptized by heretics. It is assumed that eventually he was reconciled. He died on the way to a synod of bishops around 268 or 269. In his most famous letter, to Cyprian, he laments the activity of a demon-possessed woman who pretended to celebrate the Eucharist in his diocese. Oddly, this text has received much attention in recent years from advocates of women's ordination.

The excerpt below is based on the translation of Cyprian's correspondence in the 1892 Edinburgh edition of the Fathers.

A Blasphemous Oath

A severe persecution arose against us who are called Christian. It came suddenly, after the long peace of the previous age, and it came with unusual evils that made it more terrifying to our people. Serenianus was then governor in our province, a bitter and terrible persecutor. The faithful were so disturbed that they fled near and far for fear of persecution, and they left their country for other regions. There was ample opportunity for escape, as persecution was local and not worldwide.

Then, suddenly, there arose among us a certain woman, who in a state of ecstasy announced herself as a prophetess, and acted as if she were filled with the Holy Spirit, when actually she was moved by the prompting of the principal demons. For a long time she upset and deceived the brethren, working miracles and portents, and promised that she would cause an earthquake. Not that the power of the demon was so great that he could prevail to shake the earth or disturb the elements; but sometimes a wicked spirit foresees that there will be an earthquake, and so he pretends that he will do what he foresees will soon come to pass. By these lies and boastings he had so tamed the minds of individuals, that they obeyed him and followed wherever he commanded and led. He would also make that woman walk in the coldest winter with bare feet over frozen snow — and not to be troubled or hurt at all. She would sometimes say that she was hurrying to Judea and Jerusalem, pretending that she had come from there. . . . That woman, who by demonic tricks and deceits, had done many things to fool the faithful. She had even dared to pretend, with the approved prayers, to consecrate bread and celebrate the Eucharist, offering sacrifice to the Lord with the accustomed utterance. She also baptized many, using the usual and lawful words of interrogation, so that nothing might seem to be different from the ecclesiastical rule.

— Preserved as Letter 75 in Cyprian's
Correspondence

CHAPTER 25

The *Liturgy of Addai and Mari*

The East Syrian *Liturgy of Addai and Mari* is an enigma to those who study history. Tradition attributes its authorship to the founders of the Church in Edessa. Addai (Thaddeus) was said to be one of the seventy-two original disciples appointed by Jesus. Mari was a man converted by Addai and ordained by him for missionary work along the Tigris River.

Edessa (modern Urfa in Turkey) was a major center of Christian culture, and some scholars believe that the *Liturgy of Addai and Mari* does contain the city's earliest liturgy. History, however, records no references to the text until the fifth century — which leads others to believe that it is a product of the followers of Nestorius, who were excommunicated by the Church in 431. In any event, political, ecclesiastical, and geographical distances likely kept this Persian rite isolated from outside liturgical influences for several centuries.

The liturgy's eucharistic prayer (or anaphora) has posed a problem for liturgists and ecumenists in recent years, because its earliest manuscripts contain no account of the institution of the Eucharist at the Last Supper. Many western theologians have argued that the institution narrative, with its words of consecration, are necessary for a valid Eucharist. In 2001, however, Pope John Paul II approved the rites of Addai and Mari — without the institution narrative — for use in Catholic churches in the east, and for common worship between Assyrian Christians and Chaldean Catholics.

Some say that the absence of the narrative is evidence of the liturgy's antiquity, as the earliest texts of all the pre-Nicene liturgies have no institution narratives (Taft 2003). Others hold that the narrative was omitted from those early manuscripts in deference to the discipline of the secret.

Use of the *Liturgy of Addai and Mari* spread with Nestorian missionaries, who evangelized areas of Iran, Iraq, India, Egypt, and China. Many eastern churches continue to use the liturgy today, including the Malabar and Chaldean rites of the Catholic Church.

The anaphora, below, is gleaned from the 1892 Edinburgh edition of the Fathers, with amendments based on some later scholarship.

The Anaphora

Priest: Worthy of glory from every mouth, and of thanksgiving from all tongues, and of worship and exaltation from all creatures, is the adorable and glorious name of Father, Son, and Holy Spirit. You created the world through your grace and its inhabitants through your mercy. You saved men through your mercy, and showed great grace toward mortals. Your majesty, O Lord, thousands of thousands of heavenly spirits, and ten thousand myriads of holy angels, hosts of spirits, ministers of fire and spirit, bless and adore. With the holy cherubim and the spiritual seraphim, they bless and celebrate your name, crying and praising, without ceasing, unto each other.

All say with a loud voice: Holy, holy, holy, Lord God Almighty! Heaven and earth are full of his glory!

The priest says in secret: Holy, holy, holy are you, O Lord God Almighty; heaven and earth are full of his praises and the nature of his essence, as they are glorious with the honor of his splendor.

And with those heavenly powers we give you thanks, even we, your insignificant, frail, and miserable servants, because you have granted us your great grace, which cannot be repaid. For indeed you took upon yourself our human nature, that you might bestow life on us through your divinity. You have exalted our low condition. You raised our ruined state; you raised up our mortality. You washed away our sins. You blotted out the guilt of our sins. You enlightened our intelligence, and you condemned our enemy, O Lord our God. You caused the insignificance of our frail nature to triumph through the tender mercies of your grace. For all your help and your favors to us, we give you praise, honor, thanksgiving, and adoration, now, always, and for ever and ever.

All: Amen.

Deacon: In your minds, pray. Peace be with you.

Priest: O Lord, through your many and ineffable mercies, make this memorial good and acceptable, with that of all the pious and righteous fathers who have been pleading before you in the commemoration of the body and blood of your Christ, which we offer to you upon your pure and holy altar, as you taught us. Grant unto us your peace all the days of this life.

May all the inhabitants of the earth come to know you, that you are the only true God and Father, and you sent our Lord Jesus Christ, your Son and your beloved. He, our Lord and God, came and taught us all the purity and holiness of the prophets, apostles, martyrs, confessors, bishops, doctors, priests, deacons, and all the sons of the holy catholic Church who have been marked with the sign of life, of holy baptism.

We, too, O Lord — your degraded, weak, and feeble servants who are gathered in your name and now stand before you — we have received with joy the rite that comes from you. We praise and glorify, exalt, commemorate, and celebrate this great, awesome, holy, and divine mystery of the passion, death, burial, and resurrection of our Lord and Savior Jesus Christ.

May your Holy Spirit come, O Lord, and rest upon this oblation offered by your servants. May he bless and sanctify it; and may it win for us, O Lord, the forgiveness of our offenses, the remission of our sins, the great hope of resurrection from the dead, and a new life in the kingdom of heaven, with all who have pleased you.

Because of your wonderful plan for us, we shall give you thanks and glorify you without ceasing in your Church, redeemed by the precious blood of your Christ. With open mouths and joyful countenances, we give praise, honor, thanksgiving, and adoration to your holy, loving, and life-giving name, now, always, and for ever.

All: Amen.

CHAPTER 26

Eusebius of Caesarea

Eusebius is Christian antiquity's first great historian, and he was himself a firsthand witness of many of history's great events. He was imprisoned in the final and most brutal persecution of imperial Rome, the persecution of Diocletian. Later, as bishop of Caesarea in Palestine, he played a pivotal role in the controversy over Arianism; and he was an active participant at the Council of Nicea (A.D. 325). Eusebius was also a sometime counselor to the court of Constantine, the emperor who legalized Christianity.

Eusebius was a thorough and remarkably critical researcher. He traveled widely to study Christianity's primary documents. His quotations often provide us the only record we have of these early texts.

But Eusebius is a complicated character. He was initially warm to the teaching of the arch-heretic Arius, though he accepted the decisions of the Council and even voted in favor of Arius's condemnation. Still, in the creeds and pronouncements that followed Nicea, Eusebius favored a language of compromise, so that Arius's followers might find it easier to return to the Church. He considered Athanasius a fanatic and worked to bring about the exile of the great "Father of Orthodoxy" from his see of Alexandria.

Eusebius composed his *Church History* in several stages and several editions over the course of his life. His history provides us many glimpses of liturgical practice, devotional art and architecture.

Earlier in life, probably before A.D. 311, Eusebius composed important works of apologetics to confront the challenges of different groups of non-Christians. In his *Demonstration of the Gospel*, he set out to prove, from the testimony of the Old Testament, that Jesus was the Messiah awaited by the Jews. In the passage included here, Eusebius treats the eucharistic liturgy as central to Christ's work of salvation.

The excerpt below is based on the translation of W. J. Ferrar (1920).

A Blasphemous Oath

According to the witness of the prophets, the great and precious ransom has been found for Jews and Greeks alike — the atoning sacrifice for the whole world, the life given for the life of all men, the pure offering for every stain and sin, the Lamb of God, the holy sheep dear to God, the Lamb that was foretold. By his inspired and mystic teaching all of us gentiles have procured the forgiveness of our former sins, and those Jews who hope in him are freed from the curse of Moses. Daily celebrating his memorial, the remembrance of his body and blood, we are admitted to a greater sacrifice than that of the ancient law. We do not deem it right to fall back upon the first impoverished elements, which are symbols and likenesses but do not contain the truth itself. And any Jews, of course, who have taken refuge in Christ are free from the curse ordained by Moses, even if they no longer keep the ordinances of Moses, but live according to the new covenant. For the Lamb of God has not only taken on himself the sin of the world, but also the curse involved in the breach of the commandments of Moses as well. The Lamb of God is made both sin and curse — sin for the sinners in the world, and curse for those remaining in all the things written in Moses' law. And so the Apostle says: "Christ redeemed us from the curse of the law, having become a curse for us" (Gal 3:13); and "For our sake he made him to be sin who knew no sin" (2 Cor 5:21). For what is there that the offering for the whole world could not bring about? The life given for the life of sinners, he was led as a lamb to the slaughter, and as a lamb to the sacrifice — and all this for us and on our behalf! . . . And after all this, when he had offered such a wondrous offering and choice victim to the Father, and sacrificed for the salvation of us all, he delivered a memorial to us to offer to God continually instead of a sacrifice.

Inspired by the Holy Spirit to foresee the future, wondrous David foretold . . .

> "Sacrifice and offering you did not desire;
> but you have given me an open ear.
> Burnt offering and sin offering
> you have not required.
> Then I said, "Lo, I come;
> in the roll of the book it is written of me;
> I delight to do your will, O my God;
> your law is within my heart" (Ps 40:6-8).

Then he adds: "I have told the glad news of deliverance in the great congregation." Thus he plainly teaches that, in place of the ancient sacrifices and whole burnt-offerings, the incarnate presence of Christ was offered. And this very thing he proclaims to his Church as a great mystery expressed with prophetic voice in the volume of the book. We have received a memorial of this offering, which we celebrate on a table by means of symbols of his body and saving blood, according to the laws of the new covenant. And we are taught again by the prophet David to say: "You have prepared a table for me in the sight of my enemies. You have anointed my head with oil, my cup overflows" (Ps 23:5). Here it is plainly the mystic chrism and the holy sacrifice of Christ's Table that are meant. By these we are taught, all through our lives, to offer to almighty God, through our great high priest, the celebration of our sacrifices — bloodless, reasonable, and well-pleasing to him. And this very thing the great prophet Isaiah wonderfully foreknew and foretold, by the Holy Spirit: "O Lord God, I will glorify you, I will sing to your name; for you have done wonderful things" (Is 25:1, *Septuagint*).

And he goes on to explain what these truly "wonderful things" are: "And the Lord of hosts shall make a feast for all the nations: on this mount they shall drink gladness, they shall drink wine: they shall anoint themselves with ointment in this mountain. Tell these things to the nations; for this is God's counsel upon all the nations" (Is 25:6-7, *Septuagint*).

These were Isaiah's "wonders," the promise of the anointing with fragrant ointment, and with myrrh made not for Israel but for all nations. So through the chrism of myrrh they gained the name of Christians. But he also prophesies the "wine of joy" to the nations, mysteriously alluding to the sacrament of the new covenant of Christ, which is now openly celebrated among the nations . . .

"For from the rising of the sun to its setting my name is great among the nations, and in every place incense is offered to my name, and a pure offering" (Mal 1:11) . . .

So, then, we sacrifice and offer incense — on the one hand when we celebrate the memorial of his great sacrifice according to the mysteries he delivered to us, and bring to God the Eucharist for our salvation with holy hymns and prayers; while on the other we consecrate ourselves to him alone and to the Word his high priest, devoted to him in body and soul. Therefore, we are careful to keep our bodies pure and undefiled from all evil, and we bring our hearts purified from every passion and stain of sin, and worship him with sincere thoughts, real intention, and true beliefs. For these are more acceptable to him, so we are taught, than a multitude of sacrifices offered with blood and smoke and fat.

— *PREPARATION FOR THE GOSPEL* 1.10

Christ neither entered his priesthood in time nor sprang from the priestly tribe. Nor was he anointed with oil, nor will he ever reach the end of his priesthood. Nor will he be established only for the Jews, but for all nations. For all these reasons he is rightly said to have forsaken the priesthood of Aaron's type, and to be a priest of the order of Melchizedek. The fulfillment of the oracle is truly wondrous to one who recognizes how our Savior Jesus, the Christ of God, even now, even today, performs through his ministers sacrifices after the manner of Melchizedek. For he who was priest of the gentiles does not appear offering outward sacrifices, but as blessing Abraham with wine and bread. In the same way our Lord and Savior himself, and then all his priests among all nations, perform the spiritual sacrifice according to the customs of the Church, and with wine and bread express the mysteries of his body and saving blood. This Melchizedek foresaw by the Holy Spirit, and so he used the figures of what was to come, as the scripture of Moses witnesses.

— *Preparation for the Gospel* 5.3

CHAPTER 27

The Anaphora of St. Mark

A lexandria in Egypt was, in the first Christian centuries, the intellectual capital of the Roman Empire. It had the world's largest library and the most prestigious university and research center. The city's sizable Jewish minority had its own distinctive culture. The philosopher Philo, a contemporary of Jesus and Paul, was the Alexandrian Jews' chronicler and their brightest light. In his work on "The Contemplative Life," Philo described a semi-monastic group of Jews, called the *Therapeutai* ("Healers"), who occupied themselves with communal prayer and intense study of the Scriptures. The *Thereapeutai* met early in the morning for the hearing of the Scripture, the singing of antiphons, and a ritual meal that had a sacrificial character. Some centuries later, the Christian historian Eusebius concluded that the *Therapeutai* eventually converted to Christianity and formed the foundational generation of the Alexandrian Church (*Church History* 2.7). The Italian liturgical scholar Enrico Mazza finds Eusebius's argument possible, at least, given the similarities between Philo's description of the *Therapeutai* and what we know of later Egyptian liturgy and monasticism.

Of course, what we know of the early centuries is, quite literally, fragmentary. All we know of the Egyptian liturgies is what we can glean from a few scraps of parchment. Scholars can, however, make further hypotheses by comparing those few fragments with apparent quotations in the works of Clement, Origen, and other Egyptians — and by comparing those early portions with later manuscripts of the Alexandrian liturgy.

According to tradition, Mark the Evangelist was the first bishop of the city, and he was martyred there in A.D. 68. The liturgy of ancient Alexandria is named for him, and it is still used today by Egypt's Coptic Christians, as well as by Christians of Ethiopia.

The oldest fragment of the *Liturgy of St. Mark* is known as the Strasbourg Papyrus (after the French University where it now resides). Published in 1928, the Strasbourg Papyrus is a single, badly mutilated sheet, with writing on both sides. Experts date the papyrus itself to the mid-fourth century, but say the text may go back to the second century or even earlier (Cuming 1990: xxvii).

Other early liturgical fragments have turned up in the Egyptian desert, but none quite as old as the Strasbourg Papyrus. In the late twentieth century, Geoffrey Cuming attempted a reconstruction of the ancient Egyptian liturgy, based on the various fragments (Cuming 1990:69-70). The following translation of Strasbourg is based on that of Quasten (1935).

The Anaphora

[It is indeed proper and right . . .] to bless you by night and day . . . [Thanks] be to you who have made heaven and earth and all that is in them, the earth and all that is on the earth, the seas and rivers and all that is in them; to you who made man in your image and likeness; and has created all things in your wisdom, your true light, your Son our Lord and Savior Jesus Christ.

Through him and with him, together with the Holy Spirit, we give you thanks and offer this reasonable sacrifice, this bloodless worship, which all peoples offer you from the rising of the sun to its setting, from the north to the south, because your name is great among all nations, and in every place incense is offered to your holy name and a pure sacrifice and oblation.

We beg and beseech you, remember your holy, one, Catholic Church, all your people and all your flocks. Give heaven's peace to all our hearts, but give us as well peace in this life. [Watch over] the king of earth; and [see to it that he keeps thoughts] that are peaceful toward us and toward your holy name, over the leader . . . [and preserve in all peace our] armies, princes, and senate.

. . . [Grant us grain for planting and for] harvest. . . . for the poor among your people, for the widow and the orphan, for the stranger and the newcomer, for all of us who hope in you and who call upon your holy name.

To those who have fallen asleep grant rest of soul. Remember those whose memory we recall this day and those whose names we recite and those we do not recite; [remember as well] our orthodox holy fathers and bishops everywhere and grant that we may share the inheritance with the splendid company of your holy prophets, apostles, [and] martyrs. . . . to them now grant through our Lord and Savior, through him be glory for ever and ever.

CHAPTER 28

Council of Nicea

The Council of Nicea (A.D. 325) is considered the first Ecumenical Council — that is, a gathering of bishops convened and confirmed by proper authority and representing the Church throughout the world. The Emperor Constantine summoned this Council to settle the Arian controversy, which had reached a crisis point and was threatening to divide the empire. Arius and his followers denied the full divinity and coeternity of the Word of God. The heresy of Arianism arose alongside other similar heresies, all similar in holding that God the Son was a creature of God the Father, and that there was a time when the Son did not exist.

While the council fathers settled the doctrinal matter, they also took up a number of disciplinary questions, some related to the liturgy.

The following canons of Nicea are based on the translation of Tanner (1990).

CANON 13

Concerning those who are dying, the ancient canon law is still to be maintained, namely that those who are dying are not to be deprived of their last, most necessary *viaticum*. But if one whose life has been despaired of has been admitted to communion and has shared in the offering and is found to be numbered again among the living, he shall be among those who take part in prayer only. But as a general rule, in the case of anyone who is dying and seeks to share in the Eucharist, the bishop upon examining the matter shall give him a share in the offering.

CANON 18

It has come to the attention of this holy and great synod that in some places and cities deacons give communion to priests, although neither canon nor custom allows this, namely that those who have no authority to offer should give the body of Christ to those who do offer. Moreover it has become known that some of the deacons now receive the Eucharist even before the bishops. All these practices must be suppressed. Deacons must remain within their own limits, knowing that they are the ministers of the bishop and subordinate to the priests. Let them receive the Eucharist according to their order, after the priests, from the hands of the bishop or the priest. Nor shall permission be given for the deacons to sit among the priests, for such an arrangement is contrary to the canon and to rank. If anyone refuses to comply even after these decrees, he is to be suspended from the diaconate.

CANON 20

Since there are some who kneel on Sunday and during the season of Pentecost, this holy synod decrees that, so that the same observances may be maintained in every diocese, one should offer one's prayers to the Lord standing.

CHAPTER 29

St. Sarapion of Thmuis

We have in the *Liturgy of Sarapion* an early and beautiful example of the ancient Mass as it was offered in Egypt. Sarapion was bishop of the city of Thmuis around 339-363. He was a friend of Athanasius, whose letters to him have survived. His "prayer-book," or *Euchologion*, includes rites for many purposes and occasions. Notable is his emphasis on prayer for the dead and on anointing of the living for healing. Sarapion's eucharistic prayer includes a blessing of oils and water for sacramental anointing.

The text below is based on the translation of Wobbermin (1899).

Preface

It is proper and right to praise, to hymn, to glorify you, the uncreated Father of the only-begotten Jesus Christ. We praise you, O uncreated God, who are unsearchable, ineffable, incomprehensible by any created substance. We praise you who are known by your Son, the only-begotten. Through him you are spoken and interpreted and made known to created nature. We praise you who know the Son and reveal to the saints the glories concerning him. You are known by your begotten Word, and through him you are brought to the sight and the understanding of the saints.

We praise you, O unseen Father, giver of immortality. You are the fount of life, the fount of light, the fount of all grace and all truth, O lover of men, O lover of the poor who reconcile yourself to all, and draw all to yourself through the advent of your beloved Son. We beg you to make us living men. Give us a spirit of light, that we may know you, the true [God], and him whom you sent, Jesus Christ. Give us the Holy Spirit, that we may be able to tell forth and announce your unspeakable mysteries. May the Lord Jesus speak in us, and the Holy Spirit, and sing your glory through us.

For you are far above all principality, power, rule, and dominion, and every name that is named, not only in this world but also in that which is to come. Beside you stand a thousand thousands and myriad myriad of angels, archangels, thrones, dominions, principalities, powers. By you stand the most honorable six-winged seraphim, with two wings covering the face, and with two the feet and with two flying and crying "Holy." With them, receive also our cry of "Holy" as we say: Holy, holy, holy Lord of hosts, heaven and earth are full of your glory.

The Offering

Full is the heaven, and full is the earth of your excellent glory. Lord of hosts, fill also this sacrifice with your power and your participation: for to you have we offered this living sacrifice, this bloodless oblation. To you we have offered this bread, the likeness of the body of the only-begotten. This bread is the likeness of the holy body, because the Lord Jesus Christ, on the night he was betrayed, took bread and broke it, and gave it to his disciples, saying, "Take this, all of you, and eat it. This is my body, which is being broken for you for remission of sins." So we also make the likeness of the death by offering the bread, and beg you through this sacrifice to be reconciled to all of us and be merciful, O God of truth. And as this broken bread was scattered over the hills, and was gathered together and became one, so let your Church be gathered together from every nation and every country and every city and village and house and make one living catholic Church.

We have also offered the cup, the likeness of the blood, because the Lord Jesus Christ, taking a cup after supper, said to his own disciples, "Take this and drink. This is the new covenant, which is my blood, which is being shed for you for remission of sins." So we have also offered the cup, presenting a likeness of the blood.

O God of truth, let your holy Word come upon this bread, that the bread may become the body of the Word, and upon this cup, that the cup may become blood of the Truth; and make all who partake to receive a medicine of life for the healing of every sickness and for the strength-ening of all progress and virtue, not for condemnation, O God of truth, and not for censure and reproach. For we have invoked you, the uncreated, through the only-begotten in the Holy Spirit.

Let this people receive mercy. Let it be counted worthy of advancement. Let angels be sent forth as companions to the people for bringing the evil one to nothing and for establishment of the Church.

We intercede also on behalf of all who have been laid to rest, whose memorial we are making.

Here recite the names.

Sanctify these souls: for you know all. Sanctify all (souls) laid to rest in the Lord. And number them with all your holy powers and give them a place and a mansion in your kingdom.

Receive also the thanksgiving [Eucharist] of the people, and bless those who have offered the offerings and the thanksgivings, and grant health and soundness and cheerfulness and all advancement of soul and body to this whole people through the only-begotten Jesus Christ in the Holy Spirit; as it was and is and shall be to generations of generations and to all the ages of the ages. Amen.

After the [Lord's?] prayer comes the breaking of the bread and a prayer.

Count us worthy of this Communion, O God of truth, and make our bodies to contain purity and our souls prudence and knowledge. And make us wise, O God of compassion, by the Communion of the body and the blood, because through your only-begotten to you is the glory and the strength in the Holy Spirit, now and to all the ages of the ages. Amen.

After giving the broken bread to the priests, hands are imposed on the people.

I stretch out the hand upon this people and pray that the hand of the truth may be stretched out and blessing given to this people on account of your loving kindness, O God of compassion, and the mysteries that are present. May a hand of piety and power and sound discipline and cleanness and all holiness bless this people, and continually preserve it to advancement and improvement through your only-begotten Jesus Christ in the Holy Spirit, both now and to all the ages of the ages. Amen.

After the distribution to the people is this prayer.

We thank you, Master, that you have called those who have erred, and have taken to yourself those who have sinned, and have set aside the threat that was against us, giving indulgence by your mercy, and wiping it away by repentance, and casting it off by the knowledge that regards yourself. We give you thanks, that you have given us Communion of the body and blood. Bless us, bless this people, make us to have our portion with the body and the blood through your only-begotten Son, through whom to you is the glory and the strength in the Holy Spirit, both now and ever and to all the ages of the ages. Amen.

We bless through the name of your only-begotten Jesus Christ these creatures; we name the name of him who suffered, who was crucified, and rose again, and who sits at the right hand of the uncreated, upon this water and upon this [oil]. Grant healing power upon these creatures that every fever and every evil spirit and every sickness may depart through the drinking and the anointing, and that the partaking of these creatures may be a healing medicine, and a medicine of soundness, in the name of your only-begotten Jesus Christ, through whom to you is the glory and the strength in the Holy Spirit to all the ages of the ages. Amen.

Laying on of hands after the blessing of the water and the oil.

O loving God of truth, let the Communion of the body and the blood continue with this people. Let their bodies be living bodies and their souls be clean souls. Grant this blessing to be a keeping of their Communion, and a security to the Eucharist that has been celebrated, and make blessed all of them together and make (them) elect through your only-begotten Jesus Christ in the Holy Spirit, both now and to all the ages of the ages. Amen.

CHAPTER 30

The Liturgy of St. James

The title of this liturgy ascribes the work to the apostle James, who was the first bishop of Jerusalem. Indeed, the text seems to have originated in Jerusalem (Jungmann 1959:224), though its early history is obscure. The fourth century, however, provides commentaries and accounts of the liturgy, including two of the richest sources of liturgical information from the ancient Church: the travelogue of Egeria, a Spanish pilgrim in Jerusalem, and the catechetical lectures of Cyril of Jerusalem.

Around the year 400, the *Liturgy of St. James* was adopted as the liturgy of the patriarchal see of Antioch, an influential Christian metropolis. From there, its influence extended far among Christians who spoke Greek and those who spoke Syrian. James provided the foundation for the development of later rites, such as the liturgy attributed to John Chrysostom, which is used today by Catholics of the Byzantine rite as well as many Orthodox churches.

We have no complete early texts of the *Liturgy of St. James*. The following excerpts are taken from the 1892 Edinburgh translation of the Fathers, which was based on a later manuscript that included elements added to the liturgy in the late patristic period.

Petitions

Priest: Peace be with you.

People: And with your spirit.

Priest: The Lord bless us all, and sanctify us for the entrance and celebration of the divine and pure mysteries, giving rest to the blessed souls among the good and just, by his grace and compassion, now and forever, and for all eternity. Amen.

Deacon: In peace let us pray to the Lord. For the peace that is from on high, and for God's love to man, and for the salvation of our souls, let us pray to the Lord. For peace in the whole world, for the unity of all the holy churches of God, let us pray to the Lord. For the remission of our sins, and forgiveness of our transgressions, and for our deliverance from all tribulation, wrath, danger, and distress, and from the uprising of our enemies, let us pray to the Lord.

Singers: Holy God, holy mighty, holy immortal, have mercy upon us.

Priest: O compassionate and merciful, patient, gracious, and true God, look from your prepared dwelling-place and hear us your suppliants. Deliver us from every temptation of the devil and man. Do not withhold your help from us, nor send us chastisements too heavy for our strength. For we are unable to overcome what is opposed to us. But you are able, Lord, to save us from everything that is against us. Save us, O God, from the difficulties of this world, according to your goodness, so that, drawn to your altar with a pure conscience, we may send up to you without condemnation the blessed and thrice-holy hymn, together with the heavenly powers. Having performed the service, well pleasing to you and divine, may we be counted worthy of eternal life.

Because you are holy, Lord our God, and dwell and abide in holy places, we send up the praise and the thrice-holy hymn to you, the Father, and the Son, and the Holy Spirit, now and for ever, and for all eternity.

People: Amen.

Priest: Peace be with you.

People: And with your spirit.

Singers: Alleluia.

[The liturgy proceeds with readings from the Old and New Testaments.]

Deacon: Let us all say: Lord, have mercy.

Lord Almighty, the God of our fathers: We beseech you, hear us. For the peace from on high, and for the salvation of our souls, let us pray to the Lord. For peace in the whole world, for the unity of all the holy churches of God, let us pray to the Lord. For the salvation and help of all Christ-loving people, we beseech you, hear us. For our deliverance from all tribulation, wrath, danger, distress; from captivity, bitter death; and from our iniquities, we beseech you, hear us. For the people standing and waiting for the rich and bountiful mercy that comes from you, we beseech you, be merciful and gracious.

Save your people, O Lord, and bless your inheritance. Visit your world with mercy and compassion. Exalt the horn of Christians by the power of the precious and life-giving cross. We beseech you, most merciful Lord, hear our prayer, and have mercy upon us.

People (three times): Lord, have mercy on us. . . .

Dismissal of the Unbaptized

Priest: O God, you have taught us your divine and saving oracles. Enlighten the souls of us sinners for the comprehension of the things that have been spoken here. May we be not only hearers of spiritual things, but also doers of good deeds, striving after sincere faith, blameless life, and pure conduct. In Christ Jesus our Lord, with whom you are blessed, together with your all-holy, good, and life-giving Spirit, now and always, and for ever.

People: Amen.

Priest: Peace be with you.

People: And with your spirit.

Deacon: Let us bow our heads to the Lord.

People: To you, Lord.

Priest: O Sovereign giver of life, and provider of good things: You gave mankind the blessed hope of eternal life, our Lord Jesus Christ. Count us worthy in holiness, and perfect this, your divine service, for the enjoyment of future blessedness. So that, guarded by your power at all times, and led into the light of truth, we may send up praise and thanksgiving to you, the Father, the Son, and the Holy Spirit, now and ever.

People: Amen.

Deacon: Let none of the catechumens remain, none of the unbaptized, none of those who are unable to join with us in prayer. Look at one another. The doors!

The doors! Be attentive, and let us again pray to the Lord.

Priest: Sovereign Almighty, King of Glory, you know all things before their creation. Show yourself to us who call upon you at this holy hour, and redeem us from the shame of our transgressions. Cleanse our minds and thoughts from impure desires, from worldly deceit, from all influence of the devil; and accept from the bands of us sinners this incense, as you once accepted the offering of Abel, and Noah, and Aaron, and Samuel, and of all your saints. Deliver us from every evil, and preserve us for continually pleasing, worshiping, and glorifying you, the Father, and your only-begotten Son, and your all-holy Spirit, now and always, and for ever.

Singers: Let all mortal flesh be silent, and stand with fear and trembling, and meditate nothing earthly within itself. For the King of kings and Lord of lords, Christ our God, comes forward to be sacrificed, and to be given for food to the faithful. And the bands of angels go before him with every power and dominion, the many-eyed cherubim, and the six-winged seraphim, covering their faces, and crying aloud the hymn: Alleluia, Alleluia, Alleluia. . . .

The Eucharistic Prayer

Priest: The love of the Lord and Father, the grace of the Lord and Son, and the fellowship and the gift of the Holy Spirit be with us all.

People: And with your spirit.

Priest: Let us lift up our minds and our hearts.

People: It is proper and right.

Priest: It is indeed becoming and right, proper and due, to praise you, to sing of you, to bless you, to worship you, to glorify you, to give you thanks, Maker of every creature visible and invisible, the treasure of eternal good things, the fountain of life and immortality, God and Lord of all. The highest heavens praise you, and all the host within them; the sun, and the moon, and all the choir of the stars; earth, sea, and all that is in them; Jerusalem, the heavenly assembly, and church of the firstborn that are written in heaven; spirits of just men and of prophets; souls of martyrs and of apostles; angels, archangels, thrones, dominions, principalities, and authorities, and dread powers; and the many-eyed cherubim, and the six-winged seraphim, which cover their faces with two wings, their feet with two, and with two they fly, crying one to another with unresting lips, with unceasing praises: With loud voice singing the victorious hymn of your majestic glory, crying aloud, praising, shouting, and saying:

People: Holy, holy, holy, O Lord of hosts, heaven and earth are full of your glory. Hosanna in the highest. Blessed is he who comes in the name of the Lord. Hosanna in the highest.

Priest: Lord, you are holy, King of eternity and giver of all holiness. Holy also is your only-begotten Son, our Lord Jesus Christ, by whom you have made all things. Holy also is your Holy Spirit, who searches all things, even your depths, O God. Holy are you, almighty, all-powerful, good, dread, merciful, most compassionate to your creatures; who made man from earth after your own image and likeness; who gave him the joy of paradise; and when he broke your commandment and fell away, did not disregard or desert him, O Good One, but disciplined him as a merciful father would, called him by the law, instructed him by the prophets; and afterwards sent into the world your only-begotten Son himself, our Lord Jesus Christ, that by his coming he might renew and restore your image. Having descended from heaven, and become flesh by the Holy Spirit and Mary, the Virgin Mother of God, he sojourned among men and fulfilled the plan for the salvation of our race. On the night he was betrayed, when he was about to endure his willing and life-giving death on the cross, he the sinless for us the sinners, he delivered himself up for the life and salvation of the world. Then, taking bread in his holy, pure, blameless, and immortal hands, he lifted up his eyes to heaven, and showing it to you, his God and Father, he gave thanks and prayed. He broke the bread, gave it to us, his disciples and apostles, saying:

Deacon: For the remission of sins and life everlasting.

Priest: Take, eat. This is my body, broken for you, and given for remission of sins.

People: Amen.

Priest: In the same way, after supper, he took the cup with mixed wine and water, and, lifting his eyes to heaven and presenting it to you, his God and Father, he gave thanks and prayed and blessed it. He filled it with the Holy Spirit, and gave it to us his disciples, saying, Drink this, all of you; this is my blood of the new covenant, shed for you and many, and given for the remission of sins.

People: Amen.

Priest: Do this in remembrance of me; for, as often as you eat this bread and drink this cup, you proclaim the Lord's death and confess his resurrection until he comes again.

Deacon: We believe and confess.

People: We proclaim your death, O Lord, and confess your resurrection.

Rite of Communion

Priest: Count us worthy, O loving Lord, with boldness, without condemnation, with a pure heart and a contrite spirit, with unshamed face, with sanctified lips, to dare to call upon you, the holy God, Father in heaven, and to say:

People: Our Father, who art in heaven: hallowed be your name. . . .

Priest: And lead us not into temptation, Lord, Lord of Hosts, who know our weakness, but deliver us from the evil one and his works, and from all his malice and craftiness, for the sake of your holy name, which has been placed upon our humility: For the kingdom, the power, and the glory are yours, Father, Son, and Holy Spirit, now and for ever.

People: Amen.

Priest: Peace be with you.

People: And with your spirit.

Deacon: Let us bow our heads to the Lord.

People: To you, O Lord.

Priest: To you, O Lord, we your servants have bowed our heads before your holy altar, waiting for the rich mercies that come from you. Send forth upon us, O Lord, your bountiful grace and blessing. Sanctify our souls, bodies, and spirits, that we may become worthy communicants and partakers of your holy mysteries, for the forgiveness of sins and life everlasting. For you are adorable and glorified, our God, and your only-begotten Son, and your all-holy Spirit, now and for ever.

People: Amen.

Priest: The grace and the mercies of the holy and consubstantial, uncreated and adorable Trinity be with us all.

People: And with your spirit.

Deacon: In the fear of God, let us attend.

Priest: O holy Lord, who abide in holy places, sanctify us by the word of your grace, and by the visitation of your all-holy Spirit. For you, O Lord, have said, you will be holy, for I am holy. O Lord our God, incomprehensible Word of God, one in substance with the Father and the Holy Spirit, co-eternal and indivisible, accept the pure hymn, in your holy and bloodless sacrifices; with the cherubim, and seraphim, and from me, a sinful man, crying and saying: Holy things for the holy!

People: One only is holy, one Lord Jesus Christ, to the glory of God the Father, to whom be glory to all eternity.

Deacon: For the remission of our sins and the propitiation of our souls, and for every soul in tribulation and distress needing the mercy and help of God, and for the return of the erring, the healing of the sick, the deliverance of the captives, the rest of our fathers and brethren who have fallen asleep beforehand, let us all say fervently: Lord, have mercy.

People: Lord, have mercy.

Then the priest breaks the bread, and holds the half in his right hand, and the half in his left, and dips that in his right hand in the chalice, saying:

The union of the all-holy body and precious blood of our Lord and God and Savior, Jesus Christ.

Then he makes the sign of the cross on that in his left hand; then, with that which has been signed, the other half. Then he begins to divide, and before all to give to each chalice a single piece, saying:

It has been made one, and sanctified, and perfected, in the name of the Father, and of the Son, and of the Holy Spirit, now and for ever.

And when he makes the sign of the cross on the bread, he says:

Behold the Lamb of God, the Son of the Father, who takes away the sin of the world, sacrificed for the life and salvation of the world.

And when he gives a single piece to each chalice he says:

A holy portion of Christ, full of grace and truth, of the Father, and of the Holy Spirit. To him be the glory and the power to all eternity. . . .

Priest: The Lord will bless us, and keep us without condemnation for the Communion of his pure gifts, now and always, and for ever.

And when they have filled, the deacon says:

Sir, pronounce the blessing.

Priest: The Lord will bless us, and make us worthy with the pure touchings of our fingers to take the live coal, and place it upon the mouths of the faithful for the purification and renewal of their souls and bodies, now and always.

Then, O taste and see that the Lord is good; who is parted and not divided; distributed to the faithful and not expended; for the remission of sins, and life everlasting; now and always, and for ever.

Deacon: In the peace of Christ, let us sing.

Singers: O taste and see that the Lord is good.

The priest says the prayer before the Communion:

O Lord our God, the heavenly bread, the life of the universe, I have sinned against heaven and before you, and I am not worthy to partake of your pure mysteries; but as a merciful God, make me worthy by your grace, without condemnation, to partake of your holy body and precious blood, for the remission of sins, and life everlasting.

Then he distributes to the clergy, and then the deacons take the patens and the chalices for distribution to the people.

CHAPTER 31

St. Cyril of Jerusalem

By the time Cyril of Jerusalem delivered his introductory lectures on Christianity — the *Procatecheses,* the *Catecheses,* and the *Mystagogical Catecheses* — the Church had enjoyed more than a full generation of peace in the empire. Constantine had issued his decree of toleration, the Edict of Milan, in 313. By then, most of the empire was Christian. When Cyril stood before his class of catechumens — around the year 350 — he preached with a liberty and clarity we do not find in older documents.

Cyril spoke in a seemingly uninhibited way about the depths of eucharistic theology, quoting freely from the liturgical texts. He is the first teacher on documentary record to define the change in the eucharistic species as a change in substance (see Quasten 1959: III, 375). Later writers, of course, would summarize this doctrine in a single term: transubstantiation.

Cyril is also the first to attempt to pinpoint the moment in the liturgy when the change occurs. He places the consecration at the epiclesis, when the priest invokes the Holy Spirit: "The bread and wine of the Eucharist, before the invocation of the holy and adorable Trinity, were simple bread and wine; but, after the invocation, the bread becomes the body of Christ, and the wine the blood of Christ" (*Mystagogical Lecture* 1.7). The change that takes place, according to Cyril, is substantial, definitive, and lasting: "The bread of the Eucharist, after the invocation of the Holy Spirit, is no longer merely bread, but the body of Christ" (*Mystagogical Lecture* 3.3).

Cyril's fifth Mystagogical Lecture, a walk-through tour of the Jerusalem liturgy, is an invaluable source of information on worship in his time. His description and quotations correspond closely with the elements of the *Liturgy of St. James* that are included in this volume.

Though Cyril is more free than his predecessors in presenting the mysteries, he is nonetheless aware of the discipline of the secret, and he frequently reminds his listeners (and readers) of their obligation to keep silence regarding the sacraments:

> If a catechumen asks you what the teachers have said, tell him nothing. For we deliver you a mystery and a hope of the life to come. Guard the mystery for him who gives the reward. Let none ever say to you, 'How will it harm you if I know?' So, too, the sick ask for wine; but if it is given at a wrong time, it causes delirium, and two evils arise: the sick man dies, and the physician is blamed.
>
> — *Procatecheses*, Prologue 12

At the end of the same lecture, he adds a postscript: "You may put these catechetical lectures into the hands of candidates for baptism and of baptized believers, but by no means of catechumens, nor of any others who are not Christians. In this matter, you shall answer to the Lord. If you take a copy of them, write this warning out in the beginning, in the sight of the Lord" (*Procatecheses*, Prologue 17).

Historians point out that Cyril takes a "high" view of the liturgy, emphasizing its awesome and even fearful qualities.

This, some say, is a peculiar characteristic of the mid- to late-fourth century, when the Church, finally at peace with the empire, was battling a rapidly spreading and corrosive rationalism in its own ranks: the Arian heresy. Whereas the Arians taught that Jesus was merely a creature (though the most important creature), the Church, through its liturgy, emphasized his godhead, his uncreated and eternal divinity.

Yet awe was hardly a novelty in the fourth century, and a profound reverence for the Eucharist pervades the works of many earlier Fathers, most especially Origen and Hippolytus. The *Didascalia,* too, in urging believers to revere the poor as they revere the altar, assumes a deep sense of piety toward liturgical objects.

Against the new wave of unbelieving rationalism, Cyril presented a mystical realism — a doctrine that saw spiritual realities pervading earthly matter and material things radically transformed by the touch of heaven.

This mystical vision was surely a consolation to him throughout his difficult episcopacy. Though he was bishop of Jerusalem for more than forty years, he spent half those years in exile, hounded at once by Arian heretics and by orthodox bishops who suspected him of the Arian heresy.

As with many early Church sources, there are intense disputes over Cyril's authorship of the works attributed to him, most especially those works included here. Some believe they were actually written by Cyril's successor as bishop of Jerusalem, John. Others hold that they are the product of a collaboration across generations — John working from Cyril's notes.

Cyril's lectures show us a Church just beginning to peek out from its hiding place. In the decades to follow, the genre of catechetical lectures — once a hidden matter — would show great developments. In the later fourth century, Ambrose of

Milan did for the Western liturgy what Cyril had done for the East, and he showed a more-than-passing familiarity with Cyril's work. A distinctive development in Ambrose's work is his mystical comparison of eucharistic communion with conjugal love. The genre of catechetical lectures, always culminating in liturgical commentary, would reach its zenith in the works of Augustine of Hippo in the West and John Chrysostom in the East.

The following excerpts are adapted from the 1892 Edinburgh edition of the Fathers.

The Real Presence

Even by itself, the teaching of blessed Paul is enough to give you full confidence concerning the divine mysteries, of which you have been found worthy, and by which you have come to share one body and blood with Christ. For you have just heard him say, quite clearly, that our Lord Jesus Christ, on the night he was betrayed, took bread; and, when he had given thanks, he broke it, and gave it to his disciples, saying, "Take, eat, this is my body." Then, after taking the cup and giving thanks, he said, "Take, drink, this is my blood" (see 1 Cor 11:23-25). Since he himself declared of the bread, "This is my body," who shall dare to doubt any longer? And since he himself affirmed, "This is my blood," who shall ever hesitate, saying that it is not his blood?

Once, in Cana of Galilee (see Jn 2:1-11), he turned water into wine, resembling blood. Is it incredible, then, that he should have turned wine into blood? When called to a bodily marriage, he miraculously worked that wonder. Shall he not rather be acknowledged to have given the fruit of his body and blood to the children of the bridal chamber?

So, with complete confidence, let us partake as of the body and blood of Christ. For in the figure of bread his body is given to you, and in the figure of wine his blood; so that, by partaking of the body and blood of Christ, you may become one body and blood with him. Thus, we come to bear Christ in us, because his body and blood are distributed through our members. According to blessed Peter, we became "partakers of the divine nature" (2 Pet 1:4).

Once, Christ spoke with the Jews, saying, "Unless you eat the flesh of the Son of man and drink his blood, you have no life in you" (Jn 6:53). They did not hear his saying in a spiritual sense, and so they were offended. They drew back, supposing that he was inviting them to cannibalism.

In the Old Testament, too, there was the "bread of the presence" (see Ex 25:23-30). This, however, since it belonged to the Old Testament, has come to an end. But in the New Testament there is bread of heaven and a cup of salvation, sanctifying soul and body; for as the bread corresponds to our body, so is the Word appropriate to our soul.

So do not think of the elements as mere bread and wine. They are, according to the Lord's declaration, the body and blood of Christ. Even though your senses tell you otherwise, let faith strengthen you. Do not judge the matter from the taste, but be fully confident, from steady faith, that the body and blood of Christ have been given to you.

Let blessed David explain the meaning of this, when he says, "You prepare a table before me in the presence of my enemies" (Ps 23:5). What he means is this: "Before your coming, the evil spirits prepared a table for men, polluted and defiled and full of demonic influence; but since your coming, O Lord, you have prepared a table before me." When the man says to God, "You have prepared before me a table," what else does he mean but the mystical and spiritual table that God has prepared for us, in the presence of — that is, in opposition to — the evil spirits? And this is true, for the former table gave communion with devils, but this gives communion with God.

"You anoint my head with oil" (Ps 23:5). He anointed you with oil upon your forehead [in baptism], for the seal that you have of God; so that you may be made the engraving of the signet (see Sir 45:12), the sanctuary of God.

"My cup overflows" (Ps 23:5). This is the cup that Jesus took in his hands, and gave thanks, saying, "This is my blood, which is shed for many for the remission of sins" (Mt 26:28).

Solomon, too, hinting at this grace, says in Ecclesiastes (9:7-8), "Go, eat your bread with enjoyment." Go, he calls, with the call to salvation and blessing, "and drink your wine with a merry heart" (that is, the spiritual wine); and let oil be poured out upon your head (you see, he alludes even to the mystic chrism); and "let your garments be always white," for the Lord is well pleased with your works; for before you came to baptism, your works were vanity of vanities (Eccles 1:2). But now, having put off your old garments and put on those that are spiritually white, you must be continually robed in white. Of course we do not mean that you are always, literally, to wear white clothing; but you must be clad in the garments that are truly white, shining, and spiritual, so that you may say with the blessed Isaiah, "My soul shall exult in my God; for he has clothed me with the garments of salvation, he has covered me with the robe of righteousness" (Is 61:10).

You have learned these things, so be fully assured. What seems to be bread is not bread, though it tastes like bread, but the body of Christ. And what seems to be wine is not wine, though it tastes like wine, but the blood of Christ. David sang of this long ago, saying: "[wine to gladden the heart of man,] oil to make his face shine, and bread to strengthen man's heart" (Ps 104:15). Strengthen your heart, then, by partaking of this bread as spiritual. And make your face shine, so that, having it unveiled with a pure conscience, you may, like a mirror, reflect the glory of the Lord, and proceed from glory to glory, in Christ Jesus our Lord. To him be honor, and might, and glory, for ever and ever. Amen.

— *MYSTAGOGICAL LECTURE* 4

A Guide to the Liturgy

By the mercy of God, you have heard enough at our earlier meetings concerning baptism and chrism, and the partaking of the body and blood of Christ. Now it is necessary to move on to what is next in order. Today we set the crown on the spiritual building of your edification.

You have seen the deacon who gives the priest water for washing, and to priests who stand around God's altar. The deacon gives water not because of bodily defilement; it is not that. We did not enter the Church with defiled bodies. Rather, the washing of hands is a symbol that you ought to be pure from all sinful and unlawful deeds. Since the hands are a symbol of action, by washing them we signify the purity and blamelessness of our conduct. Did you not hear the blessed David opening this very mystery, and saying, "I wash my hands in innocence, and go about your altar, O Lord" (Ps 26:6)? The washing of hands is a symbol of immunity from sin.

Then the deacon cries aloud, "Receive one another, and let us kiss one another." Do not think that this kiss is like those given in public by common friends. No, this kiss blends souls one with another and pledges mutual, wholehearted forgiveness. The kiss is the sign that our souls are mingled together, as we banish all grudges. This is why Christ said, "If you are offering your gift at the altar, and there remember that your brother has something against you, leave your gift there before the altar and go; first be reconciled to your brother, and then come and offer your gift" (Mt 5:23-24). The kiss is reconciliation, and so it is holy: as the blessed Paul said somewhere, "Greet one another with a holy kiss" (1 Cor 16:20); and Peter, with a kiss of charity (1 Pet 3:15).

After this, the priest cries aloud, "Lift up your hearts." For truly, in that most awesome hour, we should have our hearts on high with God, and not below, thinking of earth and earthly things. In effect, the priest invites everyone, in that hour, to dismiss all cares of this life, or household anxieties, and to have their hearts in heaven with the merciful God.

Then you give your agreement by answering, "We lift them up to the Lord." But let no one come here who could say with his mouth, "We lift up our hearts unto the Lord," while his thoughts were really concerned with the cares of this life. We should always keep God in mind; but if human weakness prevents this, we should at least make our best effort during that hour.

Then the priest says, "Let us give thanks to the Lord." Truly we have a duty to give thanks, because he called us to such great grace, though we were unworthy; because he reconciled us when we were his enemies; because he gave us the Spirit of adoption.

Then you say, "It is proper and right." For in giving thanks we do something that is proper and just. He, for his part, exceeded mere justice in doing us good and finding us worthy of such great benefits.

After this, we mention heaven, earth, sea, sun, moon, stars, and all creation, rational and irrational, visible and invisible; as well as angels, archangels, virtues, dominions, principalities, powers, thrones, and the cherubim with many faces. In effect, we repeat the call of David: "Magnify the Lord with me" (Ps 34:3). We make mention also of the seraphim, whom Isaiah, in the Holy Spirit, saw standing around the throne of God, each with two wings veiling his face, while with two he covered his feet, and with two he flew, crying, "Holy, holy, holy is the Lord of Hosts" (see Is 6:2-3). We recite this confession, delivered to us from the seraphim, so that we may join the armies of the world above in their hymn of praise.

After sanctifying ourselves by these spiritual hymns, we beg the merciful God to send forth his Holy Spirit upon the gifts lying before him; that he may make the bread the body of Christ, and the wine the blood of Christ; for whatever the Holy Spirit touches is surely sanctified and changed.

Then, after the spiritual sacrifice, the bloodless service, is completed, over that sacrifice of propitiation, we beg God for the common peace of the churches, for the welfare of the world; for kings; for soldiers and allies; for the sick; for the afflicted; and for all who need help, we pray and offer this sacrifice.

Next we remember those who have fallen asleep before us: first, patriarchs, prophets, apostles, martyrs, that by their prayers and intercessions God would receive our petition. Then, we pray for the holy fathers and bishops who have fallen asleep before us and all who in past years have fallen asleep among us. We believe it will be a great benefit to the souls for whom the prayer is raised during that holy and most awesome sacrifice.

Let me show you an illustration. I know that many say, "What good can prayers do for a soul that has departed this world, either with sins or without sins?" If a king were to banish certain people who had offended him, but then their families should weave a crown and offer it to him on behalf of those under punishment, would he not grant a remission of their penalties? In the same way, when we offer our supplications for those who have fallen asleep — even if they were sinners — we weave no crown, but offer up Christ sacrificed for our sins, propitiating our merciful God for them and for ourselves.

After these things, we say that prayer that the Savior gave to his disciples. With a pure conscience, we call God "our Father" as we say, "Our Father, who art in heaven." How great is the mercy of God! On those who rebelled against him and were reduced to utter misery he has bestowed such a complete forgiveness of evil deeds, and so great a portion of grace, that they should even call him Father — our Father, who art in heaven! They, too, are a heaven who bear the image of the heavenly man, since God dwells in them and walks with them (see 1 Cor 15:49).

"Hallowed be thy name." The name of God is by nature holy, whether we say so or not; but since it is sometimes profaned among sinners — as the saying goes, "Through you my name is continually blasphemed among the Gentiles" (see Is 52:5) — we pray that in us God's name may be hallowed. Not that it becomes holy after not being holy, but because it becomes holy within us, when we are made holy, and do things worthy of holiness.

"Thy kingdom come." A pure soul can say with boldness, "Thy kingdom come." He who has heard Paul saying, "Let not sin therefore reign in your mortal bodies" (Rom 6:12), and has cleansed himself in deed, thought, and word, will say to God, "Thy kingdom come."

"Thy will be done on earth as it is in heaven." God's divine and blessed angels do the will of God, as David said in the psalm, "Bless the Lord, O you his angels, you mighty ones who do his word" (Ps 103:20). So, in effect, you mean this by your prayer, "As in the angels your will is done, so let it be done on earth in me, O Lord."

"Give us this day our [daily] substantial bread." Common bread is not substantial, but this holy bread is substantial, as it is appointed for the substance of the soul. This bread goes not into the belly to be passed into the drain (see Mt 15:17), but is distributed into your whole system for the benefit of body and soul. By "this day," he means "each day," as also Paul said, "while it is called today" (see Heb 3:15).

"And forgive us our trespasses as we forgive those who trespass against us." For we have many sins! We offend in word and in thought, and we do many things worthy of condemnation. As John says, "If we say that we have no sin, we lie" (see 1 Jn 1:8). So we make a covenant with God, begging him to forgive our sins, as we also forgive our neighbors' sins. Keeping in mind the disproportion between what we receive and what we give, let us not delay forgiving one another. The offenses committed against us are slight and trivial and easily settled. But those that we have committed against God are great, and need such mercy as only he can give. Take care, then, lest, for the sake of some slight and trivial sins, you shut out God's forgiveness for your very grievous sins.

"And lead us not into temptation, O Lord." Is the Lord teaching us to pray that we may not be tempted at all? Why, then, does it say elsewhere [in Tertullian], "A man untempted is a man unproved"? And again, "Count it all joy, my brethren, when you meet various trials" (Jas 1:2)? Does entering into temptation mean being overwhelmed by temptation? Temptation is like a winter storm, difficult to cross. Those who are not overwhelmed by temptations pass through, showing themselves to be excellent swimmers, who are not swept away by the tide. Those who are of the other sort enter into the temptations and are overwhelmed. Judas, for example, entered into the temptation of the love of money. He did not swim through it, but was overwhelmed and was strangled, both in body and spirit. Peter entered into the temptation of denial; but, having entered, he was not overwhelmed by it, but courageously swam through it, and was delivered from the temptation. Listen again, in another place, to a company of unscathed saints, giving thanks for deliverance from temptation: "You, O God, have tested us; you have tried us as silver is tried. You brought us into the net; you laid afflictions on our loins. You let men ride over our heads; we went through fire and through water; and you have brought us forth to a spacious place" (Ps 66:10-12). You see them speaking boldly of having passed through and not been pierced. But "you have brought us forth to a spacious place." Their arrival at a place of rest is their deliverance from temptation.

"But deliver us from evil." If "Lead us not into temptation" implied not being tempted at all, he would not have said, "But deliver us from evil." Now, "evil" is our adversary, the devil, from whom we pray to be delivered.

Then, after completing the prayer, you say, "Amen." By this Amen, which means "So be it," you set your signature to the petitions of the divinely taught prayer.

After this, the priest says, "Holy things for the holy!" Holy are the gifts presented, having received the visitation of the Holy Spirit. Holy are you, too, who have been found worthy of the Holy Spirit. The holy things, therefore, correspond to the holy persons. Then you say, "One is Holy, One is the Lord, Jesus Christ." For One is truly holy by nature. We are holy, but only by participation, discipline, and prayer — not by nature.

Next you hear the cantor inviting you, with a sacred melody, to the communion of the holy mysteries, and saying, "O taste and see that the Lord is good." Trust not the judgment of your tongue, but rather unwavering faith. For those who taste are invited to taste, not bread and wine, but the fulfillment of the types, the body and blood of Christ.

In approaching, then, do not extend your wrists or spread your fingers; but make your left hand a throne for the right, as if to receive a King. Then hollow your palm, and receive the body of Christ, saying over it, "Amen." Then, after carefully blessing your eyes by the touch of the holy body, consume it, careful not to lose any small particle; for whatever you lose is as much a loss to you as if were one of your own limbs. Tell me, if anyone gave you grains of gold, would you not hold them with utmost care, on guard against losing any? Will you not take greater care not to lose a crumb of what is More Precious than Gold or jewels?

Then, after partaking the body of Christ, draw near to the cup of his blood — not stretching forth your hands, but bowing and reverently saying, "Amen." Then bless yourself by partaking of the blood of Christ. And while the moisture is still upon your lips, touch it with your hands, and bless your eyes and forehead and the other organs of sense. Then wait for the prayer and give thanks unto God, who has counted you worthy of such great mysteries.

Keep these traditions undefiled, and keep yourselves free from offense. Never cut yourselves off from Communion; never let yourselves be deprived, through the pollution of sin, of these holy and spiritual mysteries.

May the God of peace sanctify you completely; and may your spirit, soul, and body be preserved entire without blame at the coming of our Lord Jesus Christ. To him be glory, honor, and might, with the Father and the Holy Spirit, now and for ever, world without end. Amen.

— *Mystagogical Lecture* 5

PART III

The Mass of the Early Christians

CHAPTER 32

Bread of Heaven in Jesus Christ: An Imaginative Venture

By all appearances, you are an ordinary resident of your town, a port in the empire's North African provinces. Nothing in your dress, speech, dwelling, or everyday work would set you apart from your neighbors who do not worship Jesus Christ. You come from a family of craftsmen; your home is neither rich nor poor, but you find it comfortable.

It is Sunday, however, and so you rise unusually early. The house is dark, as is the street outside. Sunrise is still hours away.

It is the Lord's day, the day each week when you commemorate the resurrection of Jesus — and you recall your own entry into the Church of Christ, on Easter Vigil some seven years ago. You pray the words of the psalm: "This is the day the Lord has made. Let us rejoice and be glad in it."

Quietly, then, you wake the other members of your family. Each rises, in turn, to dress in the dark. A lighted window, after all, could draw unwelcome attention from the deputies of the governor. From the dockworkers you have heard rumors of persecution abroad and wonder if your town might be next.

Once dressed and washed, you and each member of your family take a small loaf of bread from the basket by the door, wrap it in a linen cloth, and then leave the house, one by one, and silently slip through the narrow streets. Though you all have a common destination, less than a mile away, you travel by different routes — again, so that you do not attract attention.

Along the way, you have only one real fright — a sudden scuttling sound behind you. It turns out to be a rat racing from the sewer in the middle of the street.

When you find yourself amid the town's larger homes, you begin to feel the familiar sense of relief and expectation. Here, at last, is the house where the Church assembles.

Even in the dark, the building is imposing. It is the ancestral home of one of the town's leading families, whose patriarch converted, with his wife and their children, just a year before you did. Though the family still lives there, the home has been increasingly turned over to the life and work of the Church. The bishop, too, lives in this house, as do some of his priests and deacons. Priests say Mass there every day, though most of the people can attend only on Sunday, as God's law requires. The risk is too great and, for many, the distance too far.

You tap your knuckles three times on the door, which opens to reveal the face of Thomas, a dockworker who is a deacon of the Church. Thomas recognizes you and lets you into the house's large entryway. Actually, it is a long, broad corridor, lit only by a few flickering lamps. There are perhaps a hundred people there already, some seated on small benches, but most standing. Everyone has an accustomed place. Consecrated virgins — women who have dedicated their lives entirely to prayer and study — occupy an area close to the front. Across the aisle from these women are several confessors who have suffered for the faith in other cities and later found refuge with your Church. Some of the confessors are badly scarred; one man is missing three fingers on his right hand.

At the back of the room stands a small group of penitents. They have sinned grievously — some are adulterers, one is a thief — but all have repented and confessed their sins before the congregation. The bishop has assigned them a penitential term, during which they may not attend the later part of the Mass; nor may they receive Holy Communion, unless they are in danger of imminent death.

Near the penitents stand the catechumens, who, during the coming Lent, will receive their first instruction in the Catholic faith. A third, small group includes men and women who have come to believe the Gospel but hesitate to present themselves for baptism, because they fear their propensity to sin again. In some places, the Church refuses readmission to any Christian who has fallen into serious sin. So some people put off baptism until a day when they feel safe from whatever particular temptation they face. Often, that day doesn't come till they are confined to their deathbed. Meanwhile, they pray that death will leave them time and won't come suddenly, as in an accident or violent attack.

Like the penitents, both these groups — the catechumens and the hesitant — will be dismissed before the eucharistic prayer begins.

Widows and orphans each have their assigned area in the congregation, as you have yours, and you find your way there. Though the room is half full, the ambience is quiet, partly from prayerful recollection, partly from sleepiness. Occasionally, a baby or a small child lets out a groggy sound before returning to the mother's breast.

As your eyes adjust to the lamplight, you see the bare outlines of the altar in the recessed alcove at the front of the room. To think that, just a few years ago, that small nook was the family's pagan shrine to their ancestors and the household gods! Now the tablinum is a sanctuary of the true God, and its wooden table is the altar of heaven.

You offer a silent prayer of thanksgiving for God's mercy, and you hear a quiet shuffling at the back of the room.

———

A deacon calls the people to be attentive. You turn to see the bishop approaching in solemn procession with his priests. At the altar, the bishop takes his seat to the right of the altar, in the finest chair. The priests take up their places, flanking the bishop on either side.

As he prays, the bishop stands with his hands outstretched, as do most of the people. To be a Christian is to pray, and to pray with the Church means to strike this posture, the *orans.* All the Christian artworks you have seen — in books, on chalices, and in paintings on the walls of homes — portray believers in this way. You, too, stretch out your arms as you respond, in your native tongue of Latin, to the prayers of the bishop.

Led by a deacon, the people raise songs of praise. Some are hymns about Jesus; others are the biblical psalms set to the local folk melodies you have known since you were a small child. The congregation sings the psalms in antiphons, the left side singing a verse, which is answered, in turn, by the right. The voices are unaccompanied in your Church, though you have heard that, in other towns, the Church sings with the accompaniment of musicians playing the lyre and kithara. So you offer a silent prayer for the conversion of musicians!

Through most of the liturgy, you and the others remain standing. The Church's few benches are kept for people who are older or ill, or for nursing mothers.

After brief introductory prayers, the bishop sits while a deacon reads from the Old Testament prophets, then the New Testament letters or the Acts of the Apostles, and finally, a story about Jesus from the Gospel.

At the close of the Gospel reading, the deacon steps aside, and the bishop walks to a place before the congregation. Now it is time for the homily, his weekly commentary and instruction based on the Scriptures. This time, he is preaching about the second reading, on the martyrdom of Stephen, and the likeness of his death to the death of Jesus. The bishop suggests that you, too, might one day face such peril. He urges the congregation to prepare for the day by praying for courage and receiving God's grace through the sacraments. He praises those Christians who have died as martyrs, as well as those present, the confessors, who have undergone cruel torture for their faith. By the end of his homily, the bishop is, by turns, rebuking those who have delayed baptism and urging them to put it off no longer.

As the bishop completes his exhortation, the deacon resumes his place and leads the prayer of the faithful. He calls the people to intercede, first, for the penitents and the catechumens. After this prayer, those groups are dismissed, and a deacon leads them to the door. The deacon continues the prayer, with petitions for the emperor and local civic leaders, for the Church, and for many other local concerns.

Sunlight is just beginning to peek in through the cracks in the curtains. The Eucharist is about to begin.

The people in the congregation turn to one another and briefly embrace, offering one another the peace of Christ. You do likewise, kissing those on either side of you on the cheek. As Jesus instructed, you make peace with your neighbor before presenting your gift at the altar.

Meanwhile, two deacons prepare the altar with fine linen and the sacred vessels. Your Church is fortunate, as another wealthy family has provided a plate and chalice of gold from their own tableware. Every Church gives its finest vessels to the Lord, but in poorer Churches, the very finest is sometimes made of glass or pottery. Yet, even then, the people decorate the vessels richly with scenes from the Scriptures.

At this point, Thomas, the deacon who watches the door, walks through the congregation holding a large basket to collect the loaves of bread. You give him yours. Some people give him flasks of wine as well. He takes the offerings to the altar, where some are placed to be consecrated. Those left over will be used to feed the priests during the coming week, and some given to the poor.

Thomas mixes wine with water in a large gold decanter and places it on the altar before returning to his place at the back of the hall.

The bishop leads the congregation in the traditional dialogue:

Bishop: The Lord be with you.
All: And with your spirit.
Bishop: Lift up your hearts.
All: We lift them up to the Lord.
Bishop: Let us give thanks to the Lord.
All: It is proper and right.

The bishop turns toward the altar, and the priests join him on either side. They are now facing the same direction you are facing — toward the east, toward sunrise, toward Jerusalem — and the bishop invites everyone to sing with the angels: "Holy, holy, holy Lord of hosts, heaven and earth are full of your glory!"

The bishop continues, then, with a long prayer giving thanks for all creation. From week to week, he rarely changes the words of this eucharistic canon. In the course of this prayer, he briefly tells the story of salvation, giving thanks for

God's mercy in every age leading up to our redemption. Then he recounts the suffering and death of Jesus. Here he tells of the Last Supper, and the bishop himself pronounces Jesus' words over the bread and wine. "This is my body. . . . This is the chalice of my blood." When the bishop brings this long prayer to a close, you join the congregation in saying, "Amen."

The bishop prays as he breaks the bread. Then, everyone, together, recites the Lord's Prayer, the Our Father. Afterward, the bishop pronounces a blessing over the people.

The congregation sings a psalm, "Taste and see the goodness of the Lord," while taking turns approaching for Communion — first the priests, then the virgins and confessors, and then the rest according to their place. When your turn comes, the bishop himself places the Body of the Lord in your hands. "The bread of heaven in Jesus Christ," he says. And you respond, "Amen."

You consume part of your portion carefully and delicately place the rest in the linen cloth in which you earlier carried your bread from home. Now that very bread has become Jesus' Body! And this portion you will reserve at home for daily Communion throughout the week.

You step aside to take the chalice from a deacon. After drinking from the chalice, you return to your usual place. When the deacons have cleared the altar, they leave with small golden boxes, called pyxes, to bear the sacrament to those who are homebound and unable to attend Mass.

But you try not to be distracted by these details. Now the Lord is with you, close to your heart! And suddenly the words of the bishop's homily come back to you, and you know that you would die for this, and that this Communion would give you strength to face such a death. Indeed, you would rather die than miss this moment. Lord, you pray, keep our persecutors far from us. But if they should find us, give us your life, that we may despise the life we are losing.

Your reverie ends abruptly as the bishop begins a final blessing, invoking God's protection during the coming week. He announces that a collection will be taken at the doors of the house. This money the Church will use for the benefit of widows and orphans, the sick, the imprisoned, and those who have been banished to the mines.

With the entire congregation, you trace the sign of the cross on your forehead as the bishop pronounces the dismissal. The people leave only gradually, in groups of two or three, and by several exits of the house. As in the darkness, now in the light, no one wants to attract undue attention.

Dropping a coin into the basket by the door, you step out into the bright morning light and hear the bustle of an ordinary business day, the clamor from the town marketplace and from the docks. Though Christians observe the Lord's day, Sunday holds no special significance for the rest of the world.

Into that world you carry the Body of Christ.

Selected References

Ambrose, St. [fourth century] 1919. *On the Mysteries and The Treatise on the Sacraments.* London: Society for Promoting Christian Knowledge (SPCK).

Aquilina, Mike. 2005. *The Fathers of the Church: An Introduction to the First Christian Teachers.* Huntington, IN: Our Sunday Visitor.

Bisconti, Fabrizio, editor. 2000. *Temi di Iconografia Paleocristiana.* Citta del Vaticano: PIAC.

Bouley, Allan, O.S.B. 1981. *From Freedom to Formula: The Evolution of the Eucharistic Prayer from Oral Improvisation to Written Texts.* Washington, DC: Catholic University of America.

Bouyer, Louis. 1968. *Eucharist: Theology and Spirituality of the Eucharistic Prayer.* Notre Dame, IN: University of Notre Dame Press.

———. 1960. *The Spirituality of the New Testament and the Fathers.* New York: Seabury.

Brightman, F.E. 1896. *Liturgies Eastern and Western.* Oxford: Clarendon Press, 1896.

Cabrol, Fernand, O.S.B. 1930. *The Prayer of the Early Christians.* Cincinnati, OH: Benziger Brothers.

———. 1934. *The Mass of the Western Rites.* Electronic edition, Internet Theology Resources, College of St. Benedict and St. John's University: www.csbsju.edu.

Cantalamessa, Raniero, O.F.M. Cap. 1993. *Easter in the Early Church.* Collegeville, MN: The Liturgical Press.

Cavaletti, Sofia. 1990. "The Jewish Roots of Christian Liturgy." In *The Jewish Roots of Christian Liturgy*, edited by Eugene J. Fisher. Mahwah, NJ: Paulist, 7ff.

Celsus [second century]. 1987. *On the True Doctrine.* Translated by R. Joseph Hoffmann. New York: Oxford University Press.

Cirlot, Felix. 1939. *The Early Eucharist*. London: SPCK.

Cullmann, Oscar. 1956. *Early Christian Worship*. London: SCM Press.

Cuming, Geoffrey J., ed. 1990. *The Liturgy of St. Mark*. Rome: Pontifical Oriental Institute.

Daly, Robert J., S.J. 1978. *Christian Sacrifice: The Judaeo–Christian Background Before Origen*. Washington, DC: Catholic University of America.

Danielou, Jean, S.J. 1956. *The Bible and the Liturgy*. Notre Dame, IN: University of Notre Dame Press.

———. 1958. *The Dead Sea Scrolls and Primitive Christianity*. Baltimore: Helicon Press.

———. 1964. *The Theology of Jewish Christianity*. Chicago: Regnery.

Davila, James R. 2000. *Liturgical Works*. Eerdmans Commentaries on the Dead Sea Scrolls, vol. 6. Grand Rapids, MI: Eerdmans.

De Lubac, Henri. 1988. *Catholicism: Christ and the Common Destiny of Man*. San Francisco: Ignatius.

Deiss, Lucien, C.S.Sp. 1979. *Springtime of the Liturgy: Liturgical Texts of the First Four Centuries*. Collegeville, MN: The Liturgical Press.

Dix, Gregory. 1945. *The Shape of the Liturgy*. London: A&C Black.

Engelbrecht, Edward. 1999. "God's Milk: An Orthodox Confession of the Eucharist." *Journal of Early Christian Studies*, vol. 7, no. 4, 509-526.

Feeley-Harnick, Gillian. 1982. *The Lord's Table: The Meaning of Food in Early Judaism and Christianity*. Washington, DC: Smithsonian Institution.

Ferguson, Everett, ed. 1998. *Encyclopedia of Early Christianity*. New York: Garland.

Ferrar, W.J., tr. 1920. *Eusebius of Caesarea: Demonstratio Evangelica*. London: SPCK.

Frend, W.H.C. 1982. *The Early Church*. Minneapolis, MN: Fortress Press.

———. 1984. *The Rise of Christianity*. Philadelphia: Fortress Press.

Frere, Walter Howard. 1938. *The Anaphora, or Great Eucharistic Prayer.* London: SPCK.

Gassner, Jerome, O.S.B. 1950. *The Canon of the Mass: Its History, Theology, and Art.* New York: Herder.

Goodenough, Erwin. 1956. *Jewish Symbols in the Greco-Roman Period.* Volumes 5-6: Fish, Bread, and Wine. New York: Pantheon Books.

Griggs. C. Wilfred. 1988. *Early Egyptian Christianity: From Its Origins to 451 C.E.* Leiden: Brill.

Hahn, Scott. 1999. *The Lamb's Supper.* New York: Doubleday.

———. 2005. *Letter and Spirit: From Written Text to Living Word in the Liturgy.* New York: Doubleday.

Hamman, Andre. 1967. *The Mass: Ancient Liturgies and Patristic Texts.* Staten Island, NY: Alba House.

———. 1961. *Early Christian Prayers.* Chicago: Regnery.

Herron, Thomas J. 1988. *The Dating of the First Epistle of Clement to the Corinthians: The Theological Basis of the Majoral View.* Rome: Pontifical Gregorian University.

Hippolytus, St. [third century] 1937. *The Apostolic Tradition.* Translated by Gregory Dix. London: SPCK.

———. 1934. *The Apostolic Tradition of Hippolytus.* Translated by Burton Scott Easton. London: Cambridge University Press.

Jensen, Robin Margaret. 2000. *Understanding Early Christian Art.* London: Routledge.

Jeremias, Joachim. 1966. *The Eucharistic Words of Jesus.* London: SCM.

Johnson, Maxwell E. 1995. *The Prayers of Sarapion of Thmuis: A Literary, Liturgical, and Theological Analysis.* Rome: Pontifical Oriental Institute.

Jones, Cheslyn, Geoffrey Wainwright, Edward Yarnold, S.J., and Paul Bradshaw, editors. 1992. *The Study of Liturgy: Revised Edition.* New York: Oxford University Press.

Jungmann, Josef A., S.J. 1959. *The Early Liturgy: To the Time of Gregory the Great.* Notre Dame, IN: University of Notre Dame Press.

———. 1964. *The Eucharistic Prayer.* Notre Dame, IN: Fides.

———. 1965. *The Place of Christ in Liturgical Prayer.* London: Geoffrey Chapman.

———. 1986. *The Mass of the Roman Rite: Its Origins and Development.* 2 vols. Allen, TX: Christian Classics.

Kodell, Jerome, O.S.B. 1991. *The Eucharist in the New Testament.* Collegeville, MN: Liturgical Press.

Koenig, John. 2000. *The Feast of the World's Redemption: Eucharistic Origins and Mission.* Harrisburg, PA: Trinity Press International.

Kollamparampil, Antony George. 2000. *From Symbol to Truth: A Syriac Understanding of the Paschal Mystery.* Roma: Centro Liturgico Vincenziano.

LaPorte, Jean. 1983. *Eucharistia in Philo.* New York: Edwin Mellen.

LaVerdiere, Eugene. 1994. *Dining in the Kingdom of God: The Origins of the Eucharist According to Luke.* Collegeville, MN: Liturgical Press.

———. 1996. *The Eucharist in the New Testament and the Early Church.* Collegeville, MN: Liturgical Press.

Mazza, Enrico. 1989. *Mystagogy: A Theology of Liturgy in the Patristic Age.* New York: Pueblo.

———. 1995. *The Origins of the Eucharistic Prayer.* Collegeville, MN: Pueblo.

———. 1999. *The Celebration of the Eucharist: The Origin of the Rite and the Development of Its Interpretation.* Collegeville, MN: Pueblo.

Musurillo, Herbert. 1962. *Symbolism and the Christian Imagination.* Baltimore: Helicon.

Nash, Thomas J. 2004. *Worthy Is the Lamb: The Biblical Roots of the Mass.* San Francisco: Ignatius.

Neusner, Jacob, editor. 1999. *Dictionary of Judaism in the Biblical Period.* Peabody, MA: Hendrickson.

Origen [third century]. 1990. *Homilies on Leviticus.* Translated by Gary Wayne Barkley. Washington, DC: The Catholic University of America Press.

Palmer, Paul F., S.J. 1963. *Sacraments and Worship: Liturgy and Doctrinal Development of Baptism, Confirmation, and the Eucharist.* Westminster, MD: Newman.

Pierse, Garrett. 1909. *The Mass in the Infant Church.* Dublin: M.H. Gill.

Pixner, Bargil, O.S.B. 1997. "Jesus and His Community: Between Essenes and Pharisees." In *Hillel and Jesus: Comparative Studies of Two Major Religious Leaders.* Minneapolis: Fortress.

Pelikan, Jaroslav. 1971. *The Emergence of the Catholic Tradition (100-600).* Chicago: University of Chicago Press.

Pusey, E.B. 1855. *The Doctrine of the Real Presence as Contained in the Fathers.* London: John Henry Parker.

Quasten, Johannes. 1935. *Monumenta Eucharistica et Liturgica Vetutissima.* Bonn: Hanstein.

———. 1952. *Patrology*, volumes I-IV. Allen, TX: Christian Classics.

———. 1973. *Music and Worship in Pagan and Christian Antiquity.* Washington, DC: National Association of Pastoral Musicians.

Ratzinger, Joseph Cardinal. 1986. *Feast of Faith.* San Francisco: Ignatius.

———. 2000. *The Spirit of the Liturgy.* San Francisco: Ignatius Press.

Robinson, John A.T. 1976. *Redating the New Testament.* Philadelphia: Fortress.

Sarapion, St. [fourth century]. 1899. *Bishop Sarapion's Prayer-Book.* Translated by G. Wobbermin. London: SPCK.

Skarsaune, Oskar. 2002. *In the Shadow of the Temple: Jewish Influences on Early Christianity.* Downers Grove, IL: InterVarsity Press.

Smith, Dennis E. 2003. *From Symposium to Eucharist: The Banquet in the Early Christian World.* Minneapolis: Fortress.

Stark, Rodney. 1997. *The Rise of Christianity.* San Francisco: HarperCollins.

Taft, Robert F., S.J. "Mass Without the Consecration?" In *America*, vol. 188, no. 16, May 12, 2003.

Tanner, Norman, S.J., ed. 1990. *Decrees of the Ecumenical Councils*, vol. 1. Washington, DC: Georgetown University.

Vermes, Geza. 1975. *The Dead Sea Scrolls in English*. New York: Penguin.

Wainwright, Geoffrey. 1981. *Eucharist and Eschatology*. New York: Oxford University Press.

Wilken, Robert L. 1984. *The Christians as the Romans Saw Them*. New Haven, CT: Yale University Press.

———. 2003. *The Spirit of Early Christian Thought: Seeking the Face of God*. New Haven, CT: Yale University Press.

———. 2001. "Angels and Archangels: The Worship of Heaven and Earth." In *Antiphon* 6 (2001).

Wise, Michael, Martin Abegg, Jr., and Edward Cook, translators. 1996. *The Dead Sea Scrolls: A New Translation*. San Francisco: HarperCollins.

Yarnold, Edward. 1994. *The Awe-Inspiring Rites of Initiation*. Collegeville, MN: Liturgical Press.

Young, Robin Darling. 2001. *In Procession Before the World: Martyrdom as Public Liturgy in Early Christianity*. Milwaukee: Marquette University Press.

Zeitlin, Solomon. 1989. "Jesus and the Last Supper." In *The Passover Haggadah*, edited by Nahum N. Glatzer. New York: Schocken, xi-xv.

For English translations of some Church Fathers, I have consulted the following series: *Ancient Christian Writers* (Mahwah, NJ: Paulist); *Fathers of the Church* (Washington, DC: Catholic University of America*); Ante-Nicene Fathers* (Peabody, MA: Hendrickson); and *Nicene and Post-Nicene Fathers* (Peabody, MA: Hendrickson).

Index

251